BASEBALL'S SERMON ON THE MOUND

Baseball's Sermon on the Mound

Frank D. Minton

BROADMAN PRESS
Nashville, Tennessee

Dedicated to

My loving wife, Joyce,

and our four children,

Bruce, Lori, Lisa, and Lesli

© Copyright 1976 • Broadman Press
All rights reserved
4255-66
ISBN: 0-8054-5566-3

Scripture quotations marked *TLB* in parentheses are from *The Living Bible, Paraphrased* (Wheaton: Tyndale House Publishers, 1971) and are used by permission.

Scripture quotations marked *TEV* in parentheses are from *The New Testament in Today's English Version* (New York: American Bible Society, 1966) and are used by permission.

Dewey Decimal Classification: 248.4
Subject Headings: Christian Life // Baseball
Library of Congress Catalog Card Number: 75-36887
Printed in the United States of America

A WORD FROM WALTER ALSTON

Frank D. Minton is a former member of the Dodger organization who has combined his baseball experiences and position as a pastor to produce an inspirational book. We think you will enjoy his efforts in his publication.

WALTER ALSTON
Manager
Los Angeles Dodgers

The Scoreboard

First Inning	"TAKE ME OUT TO THE BALL GAME"	9
Second Inning	SITTING THE BENCH	16
Third Inning	THE HOME RUN	24
Fourth Inning	KILL THE UMPIRE	33
Fifth Inning	TWIN KILLING	40
Sixth Inning	SIGN HIM UP	47
Seventh Inning	THE SEVENTH INNING STRETCH	56
Eighth Inning	THE SERMON ON THE MOUND	64
Ninth Inning	DON'T DIE ON THIRD	71
Tenth Inning	EXTRA INNINGS	79
Last Inning	AFTER TWENTY YEARS	87

Pitcher Frank Minton when he was in the Dodger organization

FIRST INNING
"Take Me Out to the Ball Game"

What sports fan has not whistled the tune, "Take Me Out to the Ball Game," at one time or another? This ever-popular tune has become a trademark for the game of baseball. In fact, no other popular song with a sports theme has so captivated the imagination of the fans.

The excitement of that catchy little lyric is seen in the expression of the pushing crowd going through the turnstiles at every baseball game; the smell of freshly-roasted peanuts and hot buttered popcorn; and the anticipation in the heart of every fan. It has helped make baseball "the great American pastime."

When I was nine years old, I viewed my first professional baseball game. It was a Pacific Coast League game between the San Diego Padres and the San Francisco Seals playing in the old wooden stadium at San Diego, California. I did not even know the difference between the shortstop and second baseman, but from my cheap seat in the bleachers, I made up my mind right then and there that I, too, would don the suit of a professional baseball player.

After years in the "sandlots," high school, American Legion, and college ranks I finally succeeded and signed a minor league contract with the Brooklyn Dodger organization. It just had to be one of the happiest days of my life. "Just think," I thought, "they are actually paying me to do what I love to do the most—play baseball!"

Almost everyone knows how to play baseball. But I found out that from the sandlots to the professional field every coach and manager has his own way to play the game.

"It is all in the way you play the game," was my first instruction when I arrived for spring training in 1955 at Vero Beach, Florida. Walter Alston was the baseball manager then, as now, and his words were eloquent on this theme.

Throughout the entire Dodger organization, it was drilled into me day after day—*sharp pitching, good defense, run the bases like lightning,* and *play to win on one run.* The wide-open home run slugging games were not the Dodgers' style of plan. They depended more on the hit and run play than the big inning backed by the home run guns.

I found in my first spring training that "take me out to the ball game" was no picnic for the professional. The fun games were over and work had set in because competition came from every corner of the United States. Young, eager ball hawks from Maine to slugging batsmen from California showed up in camp ready to take the first job available.

Competition for me as a left-handed pitcher was almost overwhelming. Back home in Kansas and Oklahoma, there were few who could overshadow my feats on the mound, but Vero Beach was a new ball game all together. I had never seen so many great left-handed pitchers in all of my life. The Dodgers were looking for a new star to bolster their pitching staff. What young pitcher with baseball fire in his bones did not dream to be "that man."

"That man" was at spring training in 1955 as a fast-balling, left-handed rookie named Sandy Koufax. Who would have thought then that this shy, unassuming personality would soon rewrite the pitching record books and become baseball's best player of the 1960's and then on to the Hall of Fame?

Sandy Koufax was just one of many competitors, so it was no wonder that the song, "Take Me Out to the Ball Game," always meant the minor leagues for me. I used to go to the ball park and sigh, "The same kind of uniform, the same five ounce baseball and look at the difference between my pitching and Sandy's." But, it was all in the way he threw that ball.

And, it is all in the way you play the game that makes baseball so exciting. The same rules, but different attitudes and strategy marks the champion over the rest of the competition.

It is the same way in life. We all live, but some succeed to the "major leagues" of life where others find themselves in the "minor leagues." Many slogans of life reach out to us to direct our way, "Eat, drink and be merry," "You've got a lot to live and we've got a lot to give," "Get all the gusto you can out of life," and "One Way Jesus," just to name a few.

There is a champion way to play baseball and a champion way to live. While I was in spring training, the Dodgers taught me the champion way to play baseball; as I have read the Bible, God has led me to know the champion way to live. Once, Jesus Christ was in the wilderness to pray and fast in preparation for his three crucial years before going to the cross. For forty days he prayed and did not eat, and he became very hungry. The devil knew of Jesus' hunger. He also knew of the plan that God had for Jesus to die on the cross to save man from sin. But the devil was determined to destroy God's plan.

So the devil came to Jesus and said, "If you are God's son, order these stones to turn into bread" (Matt. 4:3, TEV). You see, the devil was trying to tell Jesus, "Eat, drink, and be merry for tomorrow you die." But Jesus answered, "The scripture says, 'Man cannot live by bread alone, but on every word that God speaks' " (Matt. 4:4, TEV).

When I was pitching in the minors in California, our Dodger farm club acquired a brilliant young rookie. This outstanding pitcher had just been graduated from high school with a sensational pitching record. Many predicted that he was not only major league material, but was headed toward baseball stardom.

Because of the ease of success as a high schooler, this young rookie, with a great future before him, soon began to break training rules on and off the diamond. Time and again, he would break curfew at night. But his wine, women, and songs caught up with him. His pitching performance became shaky, and game by game he began playing worse instead of better. It was not long before he was sent to the lower minors never to be heard of again as a factor in professional baseball. He thought he could be a success without discipline.

The Bible is true when it states, "There is a way that seems right to me, but its end is the way to death" (Prov. 14:12, RSV).

While Jesus continued to pray in the wilderness, the devil took him to the Holy City and set him on the highest place of the Temple. "If you are God's Son, throw yourself down to the ground" (Matt. 4:6, TEV) the devil tempted.

"Jesus answered, . . . You must not put the Lord your God to the test" (Matt. 4:7, TEV). The devil was trying to get Jesus to live His life the sensational way. Of course, the devil was trying to destroy God's plan of the cross by this strategy. But Jesus again exercised a holy discipline.

During my first year of professional baseball pitching for the lowly class D Shawnee Hawks, I had a great winning year. I was always eager to read the sports page the next day. One day as I was reading the hometown newspaper about some of my baseball feats, Jack Banta, my manager, spotted me and said, "Say Frank, do you like what you're reading?"

"I sure do," was my return quip.

"You can read what the newswriters print, but you are through as a ballplayer when you begin to believe them." I never forgot his words.

The St. Louis Cardinals gave a young man a five digit bonus to pitch for them in the 1950's. His first chance came against the then world champion Dodgers. It was an overwhelming assignment for a rookie fresh out of high school. With no outs and the bases loaded, he faced those dangerous Dodgers that day in St. Louis. With machine-like rhythm and steel-like nerves, this young rookie put the great Dodgers down 1-2-3 without a run!

A new star was born in St. Louis that summer day and all the sportswriters began to turn out sensational words regarding this remarkable young pitcher. The magic continued for the rest of the season, but then the sophomore second-year slump caught up with the promising pitcher. Soon he was shipped down to the minors never to regain his poise and greatness again.

Why did not this young rookie achieve greatness? No one really knows, but one old-time scout told me, "Frank, the young man began to believe the sensational stories the sportswriters were writing about him and it ruined him." Do not let the sensational bright lights of this world blind you from playing the game of life right before God.

Again the devil approached Jesus. This time he took Jesus to a very high mountain and showed him all the kingdoms of the world, in all their greatness. "All this I will give you if you kneel down and worship me" (Matt. 4:9, TEV) promised the devil. You see, he was saying, "Let me take you out to the ball game of life, my way." Again, the devil was trying to destroy God's plan of salvation for all men.

"Then Jesus answered, 'Go away, Satan! The scripture says, 'Worship the Lord your God and serve only him!' " (Matt. 4:10, TEV).

My first college baseball win was for the University of Oklahoma against Iowa State. My Coach, Jack Baer, told me precisely how to pitch to the clean-up batter. His last words to me before the ninth inning were, "Pitch the big man high." My fast ball was blazing, and we were ahead by one run when I found myself facing the tall rangey clean-up striker. Suddenly, I forgot Coach Baer's warning. "This guy can't hit that good fast pitch of mine," I thought. Feeling overconfident, I threw my best pitch straight down the hopper into the batter's strength area.

Low and inside it sped toward the catcher and then like a rocket, the ball was slammed high into center field. It was tagged home run all the way! My heart sunk.

In the last moment, my twin brother, Fred, made a leaping one-handed stab for the ball. I can still see Fred hanging on to the top of the fence with one hand and reaching up to snatch the ball out of the air with the glove hand. It was a great moment, a spectacular save! Oklahoma 5 — Iowa State 4. But, I was almost afraid to leave the mound for I had gone against the instructions of my coach. How ashamed I was to think that I knew more than he. How wrong I was to try to play the game my way instead of following Coach Baer's instructions. Sad, but true, there are many people who feel they know more about life than God. They create their own rules, and then hope to be a winner. But every life, depending on its own strength and direction, soon tastes bitter defeat. Some even think they can do everything wrong and come out right.

Jesus knew why he was in the world. In his own words he said, "The Son of man is come to seek and to save that which was lost" (Luke 19:10), and that meant to live God's way. It was not a selfish life or a life on the loose. It meant sacrifice, discipline, and death. But the death of Jesus on the cross meant victory and life for us.

You see, the "game of life" the devil wanted Jesus to play was one of selfishness, sensationalism, and pride. This would never produce victory. Don't ever let the bright lights of the world blind you from playing the game right. You may not always get a hit every time as you come to bat in life, but because of Jesus' victory on the cross and over the grave, we can walk off the field of life a winner by trusting Jesus instead of ourselves.

So, when it comes time to "Take Me Out to the Ball Game," let us go with God.

SECOND INNING
Sitting the Bench

A Little Leaguer's Prayer

Lord, give me strength
    To hit that ball;
And if I should,
    Don't let me fall.

Help me to pick
    The one that's right;
Then let me knock it
    'Way out of sight.

Then help me run,
    With deer-like grace;
Don't let me slip,
    But tag first base.

Then on to second,
    Stay with me, Lord;
'Cause this one out,
    We can't afford.

Then let me zoom
    Like a flying bird,
Right down the line
    And on past third.

> Then let me slide,
> > With foot out-thrust;
> Across home plate,
> > Through swirling dust.
>
> But first of all,
> > Dear Lord, I pray,
> Just tell the coach
> > To let me play
>
> —Don J. Gates

No athlete of any description wants to sit the bench when the game is in full swing. The fun is in playing the game, not sitting and watching. But every great athlete has had his turn on the bench. Hall of Famer Sandy Koufax, the greatest recent-day pitcher of all, sat the bench in a Dodger uniform for nearly three years before his regular pitching days. Dodger Manager Walt Alston said of Sandy, "He wouldn't have been with us, but the league ruling about "bonus babies" kept him on the bench for his first two years." Sandy rarely got to play, and Alston was quoted, "Sandy only pitched when the game was hopelessly lost. Then, anybody would do and I mean just anybody!"

Even though you do not become a star sitting on the bench, that is where a star usually begins his career. When I began to play on my first baseball team at 13, the name of the game for me was "sitting the bench." Boy, did I want to play in a real game.

Then one day it happened! The coach let me play. Somehow, I managed to hit a grounder to short. The shortstop let it go between his legs, and I was safe at first base on an error. My twin brother, Fred, was up next and he, too, hit one that landed me on third and Fred on second. I was scared as a jack rabbit hunted by a pack of hound dogs. My heart was pounding so loudly, I thought it would jump right out of me.

Fred was on second base as scared and jumpy as I, for it was his first time in a real game, too. My coach at third base, seeing his two nervous "rookies" on the base paths for the first time in their lives, cupped his hands and hollered above the excitement and commanded, "Don't move unless I tell you, and then run!" His last words were lost in the screams of the small crowd as the next batter hit a long, high fly to left field.

"Run, Run!" screamed the overexcited coach. Down the third base line I flew toward home plate.

To the surprise of my coach, the little outfielder made an amazing catch of the fly ball. All of a sudden in the middle of the noise, my coach came running wildly toward me at home plate, screaming to the top of his lungs, "Go back—go back to third!"

Confused and excited, I ducked my head and tore back to third base for all my worth. Just as I was sliding into third base, my twin brother, Fred, came motoring around third and passed me up as he headed for home plate.

Fred slid into home plate ahead of the throw from the outfield. He thought that he had won the game. But the ump called both of us out *because Fred had passed me up at third base.* We twins were double-trouble that first game because of the double out. My first game almost ended my baseball career. So it was back to the bench where I sat for weeks.

Life is like that, too. Just as we begin to play the game, we find ourselves back on the bench. It happened to a man in the Bible. His name was John the Baptist. If he had been an athlete, he probably would have ended up in the Hall of Fame.

John the Baptist was such a great preacher that he was compared to the Old Testament prophet, Elijah. His preaching "roared like a lion," and people by the thousands came to the River Jordan to hear him.

He was the Billy Graham of his day. But more than that, John the Baptist was the forerunner of Jesus Christ. He was the first one to point to Jesus, the Savior, and say, "Here is the Lamb of God who takes away the sin of the world" (John 1:29, TEV).

But one day, John found himself "on the bench" in the religious world. Evil King Herod had put John in prison. John's preaching had become too honest for the king. In John the Baptist's fashion, he had fearlessly "taken Herod to bat" and accused him of adultery to his face.

No longer was John in the wilderness preaching. No longer was he the religious star. No longer were the crowds following him. He was "on the bench" in prison.

All alone, John the Baptist became discouraged and confused. Now, as the forgotten prophet, doubts began to creep into his mind. Things he once was so sure of became questions. "Was Jesus really the savior of the world?" he thought. He had to hear the truth once again, or go mad in his now silent stadium.

So he sent messengers to Jesus to ask, "Are you the one . . . or do we expect someone else" (Matt. 11:3, TEV).

Jesus sent back the answer, "Tell John what you are hearing and seeing: how the blind can see, the lame can walk, the lepers are made clean, the deaf hear, the dead are raised to life, and the Good News is preached to the poor. How happy is he who has no doubts about me!" (Matt. 11:4-6, TEV).

What are we to do when we are "sitting the bench" in life? Jesus tells us "Watch and Pray." In other words, "Be ready, don't just sit there."

In 1907, writer I. E. Sanborn made an observation that has become a baseball truism, "The strength of a modern major league team lies in its substitutes."

The pros do not just sit the bench idly looking at the game. The bench is literally a beehive of activity. Each man is concentrating upon every play. Each player is studied for tell-tale signs of weakness. Strategy is charted. Every player is geared and ready for instant response if the coach gives the signal to warm up and go into the game. The bench is more than sitting—it is being ready for action.

In 1952, Wichita High School North won the Kansas baseball championship. I was privileged to be a part of the team under its flamboyant coach, A. R. "Monk" Edwards.

We had a sophomore pitcher by the name of Bob who sat the bench all season long. He was fortunate to suit up as a sophomore and enjoyed his position on the team as a relaxed bench warmer.

The regional play-offs were to begin the next day. With the Kansas sun shining brightly, "Monk" gave us the warning. "Don't get sunburned because it will make your muscles stiff and sore."

But the beckoning of the warm sunshine and the prospect for a perfect day of golf was too much for Bob. So, off to the golf links went the thoughtless pitcher the day before the game. As the day warmed up and Bob's golf game became more intense, he pulled off his shirt to feel relaxed. He became so involved in chasing the little white ball over the greens he didn't notice the small burning from the sun's rays.

The next morning Bob could hardly get out of bed. His whole body seemed to be aflame. Looking into the mirror, he easily saw his problem. From the waist up he was fire-wagon red. Even the slightest touch of clothing was painful to his skin. It was then he remembered the warning from Coach "Monk" Edwards.

Bob quickly slipped into the clubhouse early that afternoon to suit up alone, so that none of his teammates would know his problem. As he attempted to put on his uniform, the shirt seemed like steel wool as he brushed it across his back. It hurt every time he moved.

Looking at his soft pitching jacket, he came across an idea. "Hmmm," he thought, "if I only wear the jacket, no one will ever know the difference." Since Bob had never gotten the chance to play all season he reasoned, "I know that all I'll do is sit the bench anyway. What difference does it make as long as I look OK?"

So, to ease the pain from the scratchy baseball shirt, Bob wore only the soft pitcher's jacket instead.

Relaxed on the bench sat the secure sophomore as the game began. Bob had somehow worked out his dilemma, and it even looked as if he were going to get away with it.

The game became lopsided toward the end. Wichita North was ahead 15 to 0. Coach "Monk" Edwards knew better than to waste his star pitcher on such poor competition, so he looked to his bullpen for a reliever.

Sure enough, there "Monk" spied his eager sophomore.

"Bob, warm up. You're next!"

Out of complete shock Bob sat motionless as if paralyzed, so suddenly came the command. Bob just sat dazed with the knowledge that he had "blown" his one great chance. The moment of truth had come. His luck had run out! Ironically, it was the very thing that Bob had worked for all season. His chance to pitch!

"Monk," seeing the petrified pitcher unable to move, went over to Bob and unzipped his jacket. There for all to see was Bob's sunburn. We were all disappointed for Bob. Even our usually unsympathetic coach felt the pathos of the moment. Bob's one great chance was gone because he wasn't ready.

"Bob," "Monk" sadly quipped, "I know you wanted to play, but you just weren't ready."

Jesus said, "Watch, and pray" (Matt. 26:41, TEV). Why? Because he is coming again to gather those who are true believers. It could be this very hour.

On that same championship high school team, we had a utility outfielder whose job for three years had been "sitting the bench." That was the name of the game for Booth. He came to every practice and every game, but he never got a chance to play.

Now Booth never did look like a baseball player. His black plastic-framed glasses made him look like the more studious type, and along with his very proper English and clear diction, he seemed a little out of place with the average baseballer. In fact, he was the chess champion of the school. But nonetheless, Booth would play as hard as the rest of us, except he wasn't quite good enough to make the first team.

In the seventh inning of a game against a cross-town rival, the score stood 2 — 1 in favor of the visitors. Our Wichita North team had two men on base, and Coach "Monk" Edwards began looking for a pinch-hitter.

Up and down he paced in front of the bench with a look of discouragement. All of a sudden, to our amazement, the proper and polite Booth stood up and begged, "Let me bat, Monk. If I don't get a hit, I'll turn in my uniform." Somehow, in that decisive moment, Booth's out-of-character plea hit its mark.

"Get in there," Monk roared, "and if you don't get a hit, take your uniform off before you come back to the bench." And the entire team knew he meant it!

Booth hurriedly selected his bat, and in a few moments was standing at the plate ready to hit anything in sight. The first pitch came whistling toward the plate. Booth swung the bat, and to our shocking surprise, hit a line shot between right and center field. It was a sure double and maybe more. By the time the center fielder could retrieve the ball, the two base runners had scored, and the amazing bench warmer had slid into third base with a triple!

The score now read 3 — 2, North High's favor.

Monk called time out and dusted off his new-found hero. "Booth," Monk happily blurted, "you never looked like a baseball player, but you're a great one in my book."

What was the difference between the two bench warmers, Bob and Booth? Bob was satisfied to sit the bench, while Booth was willing and ready to play.

Remember the words of Jesus, "Be . . . ready" (Luke 12:40).

THIRD INNING
The Home Run

At the first crack of the bat on baseball's opening day in April, the home run race is underway. It is a wonderful race with excitement, thrills, suspense and general interest that eclipses all else in baseball. Nothing brings more excitement to the crowd than to see the horsehide jump off the bat and out of the park like a streaking missile.

I hit only one home run in my brief professional career, but what a sensational feeling! Since I was a pitcher, I was not expected to do too much with the bat, but there was always that desire to "knock one outta the park."

I remember it as well as if it were yesterday. I was pitching for the Dodger's farm team in the old Class D Sooner State League with the Shawnee, Oklahoma club. We were playing against a Chicago Cub farm team from McAlester, Oklahoma. As I came to the plate, we were behind 2 − 0. The pitch came singing in and before I realized it, my bat had connected. The ball went booming its way over the scoreboard! I guess I was the most surprised guy in the stadium as I jogged around the base paths.

But to add to the excitement of that night, my twin brother, Fred, who was playing centerfield and batting in the number two slot, came up in that same inning. Gene

Wallace, our shortstop, was on second base. "Hit one like your twin brother," came the cries from the crowd in the stands. It really put my twin under pressure, but he was the man for the task. As if it were a dream come true, he, too, hit one in almost the identical spot over the scoreboard. There was sure some celebrating that day!

Yes, it has been the home run that has given new life to baseball. The 1927 Yankees would have been forgotten if it were not for the home run hitters Babe Ruth, Lou Gehrig, and Tony Lazzeri. It was one of the most destructive teams ever assembled, and received the immortal name of "Murderer's Row."

How about the 1961 Yankees who belted the "Reach" baseballs for a history-breaking round-tripper record of 240. Of that number, four men hit a total of 175 home runs: Roger Maris, 61; Mickey Mantle, 54; Bill Skowron, 28; and Yogi Berra, 22. Imagine, all "go for broke" hitters on one team. What a powerhouse!

Who will ever forget these three immortal pennant-crisis homers? Hank Greenberg's stroke for the Tigers in 1934 gave him Detroit's "favorite son" image. Gabby Hartnett's "homerun in the gloaming" for the Cubs in 1938 brought music to the streets of Chicago. And then in more recent memory, Bobby Thomson's "homer heard 'round the world" for the Giants in 1951 will always be a trophy for baseball.

The year 1974, all eyes were upon Hank Aaron of the Atlanta Braves, as he made baseball history by breaking Babe Ruth's lifetime record of 714 home runs. Hank ended the year with 725 lifetime homers. But no one, not even Hank, ever hit them more stylishly and dramatically than the Babe. He was electrifying even when he swung and missed. His missed swing would propel his body almost completely around, twisting his legs together like a pretzel. Because of this tremendous display of power, he became famous as the "Sultan of Swat" and they dubbed Yankee Stadium "The House that Ruth Built."

Even those who are not too familiar with baseball have heard of Ruth's most famous epic. It was during the 1932 series at Chicago when the Babe stepped to the plate amid a torrent of boos from the stands and the Cub's dugout. As Charley Root, the Chicago hurler, grooved the first one, Babe held up one finger for all to see. Another strike came across while his bat remained motionless, and this time Ruth held up two fingers. Then the Babe pointed to the center field fence, showing where he was going to hit the next one. Sure enough he hit the ball out of the park. Smiling from ear to ear with delight, Ruth circled the bases and gave the baseball world one of its greatest stories.

Ever since the end of World War II, the dimensions of ball parks have been shrinking because fans like to see the ball fly over the fence. When the Pittsburg Pirates obtained home run slugger Hank Greenberg from the Detroit Tigers, the Pirates created a short left field fence and called it "Greenberg Gardens." Before the 1961 season, the San Francisco Giants, long on hitting, moved in the fences of Candlestick Park, so their big guns, Willie Mays and Orlando Cepeda, could hit home runs despite the winds. "Every pitch in the upper deck" is the cry of some baseball enthusiasts who like seeing the hitter "kill the ball."

The desire to hit the home run is a wish we all possess. It is a dream within us. Who has not, in his own mind, trotted around Yankee Stadium as a "second" Babe Ruth? It is true not only in baseball, but in other endeavors of life; we desire to succeed in a big way. The spirit of going all the way and coming home a winner grips all of us at one time or another. The disciples who followed Jesus also had that "home run" blood coursing through their veins. "Who is greatest in the Kingdom of heaven?" (Matt. 18:1, TEV) came the question among themselves. You see, when Jesus was not with them, they began to argue about who was going to be the greatest in heaven. James and John, with encouragement from their mother, thought maybe they would get the coveted positions.

That hero concept many times creeps in to dominate our passions and motives in life. As I pointed out, even the disciples who followed Jesus had that problem. What might have begun with small words of pride by James and John, soon became a full-blown dispute among the twelve apostles.

Jesus never intended for his followers to have a special ranking among themselves. He did not want his "church" to get jealous over who was to be considered his closest friends. Jesus wanted them to be together as a team to do his work here on earth. It disturbed him when he knew of the pride and jealousy among them.

The 1961 home run race between the Yankees' "M and M" boys, Mickey Mantle and Roger Maris, overshadowed the entire baseball world, including the pennant and World Series. Mantle's brilliant 54 smashes were not enough to capture the home run race against Maris' record-breaking 61 homers. But for all it was worth in excitement and monetary gains, it did not really help the spirit of the club. Many reports concerning attitudes of the team members were far from the usual championship spirit.

The pressure cooker home run race of fame and success finally took its toll in the life of Roger Maris. His hair began to fall out in patches, and after each home run, his skin would break out in goose pimples. His commentary was sad for a hero, "It's good being famous, but I can't do the things I like anymore."

Baseball is so genuinely a team game that a winning team cannot rely solely on a few long ball hitters. The words "A Team Game" are in bold print. You usually can't win unless all nine players are working together. There is no place for self-pride and jealousy.

During my second year in the minor leagues, we had a good club that was predicted to take first place. Because of a personality difference, the shortstop and third baseman did not get along. The first baseman and catcher became jealous over their positions in the batting order. Two outfielders got into a fight over a ball that dropped between them when both men collided with each other. The pitchers wished each other bad luck, and to make matters worse, very few of the players liked the manager. The whole bench was in an uproar choosing sides over their friends.

Our good team soon went from bad to worse. We fell from second place to sixth in a matter of a few weeks. It was not the ability of the players that was causing the many defeats. The problem rested in the inability of the players to work together and so we became a sixth rate club.

Jesus looked intently at his disciples when they arrived at the town of Capernaum, for he knew their hearts. They could not cover up the argument they had among themselves.

"What were you arguing about on the road?" (Mark 9:33, TEV). The disciples were stunned by the question and stood before their master in silence. Jesus sat down, and said to them, "Whoever wants to be first, must place himself last of all, and be the servant of all" (Mark 9:35, TEV), "and he took a child and set him in the midst of them." Jesus was saying, "You don't have to be a home run slugger to be placed in my batting order. You don't need to 'knock it out of the park' to star on my team. You can bunt and be part of my kingdom's work."

It is interesting to note that the play of the decade for early baseball was not the home run at all, but the lowly bunt. One of the biggest bunt plays was engineered in 1910, Connie Mack's Philadelphia club, when he signaled for a *double squeeze play* which scored Rube Oldring all the way from second on a bunt by Eddie Collins. And amazing but true, John McGraw once fined one of his stars, Red Murray, $25 for taking a full swing and hitting a home run when the bunt sign was on. That was big money way back then.

During the baseball year of 1957, I was playing with the Dodger's farm club, Reno, Nevada, in the California State League. Fran Bonair was our left fielder and the most incredible hitter in baseball at that time. Fran led the entire professional baseball world with a staggering batting average of .436. He hit .435 for Hornell, New York, in 1955 to capture the title and the "Silver Bat Award" for the first time in his career. He was a slugger among sluggers.

Toward the end of the season, when every game weighed heavily for the pennant, we were one run behind the Bakersfield, California, team. With two men on base and two outs, we had the good luck of Bonair coming to the plate. Everyone in the stands cried, "Knock it outta the park."

The crowd became noisy with renewed excitement as mighty Bonair took his place at the plate. Fran glanced down at third to get Manager Ray Perry's sign. But he could hardly believe his eyes for "Little Buffalo" Perry had given the bunt signal! The puzzled Bonair stepped out of the batter's box just to be sure he was seeing right.

Again the sign was flashed by Perry, skin on skin. "Me? I can't believe it. Why, I can hit that ball over the fence," were the thoughts of the slugger. Bonair stepped up again to swing. But to the complete surprise of the Bakersfield club, he laid down a beautiful bunt along the third base line, scoring the runner at third and allowing the man on second base to advance to third. The opposing team was so "shook" by the stunning play that their catcher threw the ball into left field in his attempt to throw the runner out at third.

So, the game was won by the lowly bunt off the bat of the minor league's greatest slugger. Fran became our hero, because he was willing to forget his home run pride and sacrifice himself to win.

Jesus said, "Whoever wants to be first must place himself last of all and be the servant of all" (Mark 9:35, TEV).

Every baseball player gets the idea now and then that he can force himself to hit home runs. Baseball fans call it "swinging for the fence." But strangely enough, it produces more strikeouts than home runs. Soon a hitting slump sets in.

I can still hear my high school coach, A. R. "Monk"

Edwards, almost prayerfully yell from third base coaching box as he would instruct our "home run" hitter: "Not a hard hit, Clancy, just a sweet hit!" He was reminding the batter—"Just meet the ball."

The players know the fundamentals—if they simply meet the ball with their own natural rhythm, they will hit safely often enough. If they have power, home runs will follow. Otherwise, their timing will be bad, and they will hit even less than their average.

All of us have experienced this tendency to "force" results, even in our spiritual lives. Many times we find ourselves fretting because we can't make some sweeping "home runs" on behalf of our Lord. But he wants us to serve him where we are, with what we are. All he asks is our best—nothing less, nothing more.

"Killing the ball" to become that Home Run King won't get the job done on the field or for the Lord. "Just meeting the ball" day by day is enough.

Every day each of us needs to read the Bible, pray, tell others about Jesus, help people in the name of the Lord, and regularly attend worship services at our church. The words of Jesus are so applicable here, "Thou hast been faithful over a few things, I will make thee ruler over many things" (Matt. 25:21, KJV).

Gene Wallace, now coach at Oklahoma Baptist University, was a skinny shortstop when he broke into the minors with the Dodgers at Shawnee, Oklahoma. He was so frail that he didn't look as if he could hit the ball out of the infield. Game after game Gene would take his regular cuts at the plate. His hitting average was good but nothing sensational. Then it happened! Wallace hit one out of the park. The bench was amazed. "How did you do it?" came the question from our surprised team.

Gene reported, "nothing more than what I had done before."

Jack Banta, then manager for the Shawnee Dodgers, reinforced Wallace's discovery: "Just keep on going to the plate, and swing at the ball as usual, and you'll get your home runs." And home runs Gene Wallace collected that season! The very next year Wallace had jumped from the lowly Class D Shawnee club to the mighty AAA Montreal team—simply because he batted every time just to do his best—nothing more and nothing less.

Jesus said, "Follow me." Nothing more and nothing less.

FOURTH INNING
Kill the Umpire

"Kill the umpire—he's blind as a bat," is heard every year from the stands. Pity the poor baseball umpire. Even though he possesses the final authority on all decisions on the playing field, he still lacks a needed popularity with the players and fans alike. Most look upon these men in blue as only "necessary evils" of the game. And there seems to have been a bad name attached to umpiring from the very beginnings of the game.

"The average league umpire," said *The Chicago Tribune,* one day in 1880, "is a worthless loafer." "How long," demanded *The Cincinnati Inquirer,* in 1882, "will the public put up with Bradley's umpiring?"

Not only does the umpire receive abuse from the onlookers, and on the playing field the ump has just as bad a time of it. This was clearly shown during a game in my brief career in the minor leagues.

The Dodger's Shawnee team was hosting the Baltimore Orioles' Paris, Texas, club. Tom Sleeper, third sacker for the Dodgers, was at bat, while Bob Stanland was catching for the farm club Orioles. With the count of two balls and one strike on the batter, the ump with a booming voice called the next pitch, "Strike Two!" "What cha mean, strike?" retorted the disturbed batsman, as he stepped out of the batter's box. "It was a mile outside, and you know it!"

"You heard me," rebuffed the ump, "It was right over the corner of the plate."

Tom Sleeper continued to jaw his disapproval of the call, "Man everybody in the ball park knows it was outside." To support his opinionated view, the man in the navy blue uniform appealed to the opposing catcher. He was sure to get some backing from Stanland. "How about it, Stanland?" "You saw it, what do you think?"

But to the surprise of both the umpire and the batter, Stanland said, "Tom's right—it wasn't no strike—everybody in the ball park knows it was high and outside!"

It has become a way of baseball life to see the gyrations of expressions and gestures as manager and umpire face each other nose to nose. You would think that they were bloodthirsty looking for murder or mayhem. First-time spectators would almost believe that a riot were about to explode. And how the fans urge them on! For some this is better than the actual playing of the game.

Baseball is funny that way. Fans can make a lot of noise, let off a lot of steam, cheer and boo, but seldom really mean it.

My manager of the Reno, Nevada, Dodgers—Ray Perry— was a ferocious word attacker of umpires. This stockily-built "Little Buffalo" was quick to defend his team against any careless umpiring. But even though no one ever went after an umpire with more explosive expressions than Perry, only once did I see this little stick of dynamite ejected from the game.

After an intense debate over a close call at home plate

Ray came huffing back to the dugout and sat down next to me. When the game had returned to normal, I ventured to question my triumphant batter.

"How do you keep from being thrown out of the game? I mean, with all that it looked like from here—well, it just seemed to be too terrible."

Wiping the sweat from his forehead with a towel that was usually draped around his shoulders, Ray spit tobacco out of the side of his mouth and said, "It's not what you say but how you say it. Oh, I don't cuss them. That's not any good, but I'm not afraid to let them know what I'm thinking."

"But, Ray," I said. "You know the ump will never change his decision on a judgment play, so why do you make such a commotion of it?"

"Hmph," came back the fiery Perry. "He will think twice the next time he calls a bad play, and furthermore, the crowds eat it up. They love a little argumentary action."

The pros have their bad moments, but a special medal of bravery needs to be placed upon chests of those gallant men of blue who "ump" the little league games. Sometimes their lives look in danger, not from the ire of the Little Leaguers or coaches, but from dear "Mom" and "Dad" in the stands.

From a cow pasture in Kansas to Yankee Stadium in New York City, the cry is heard "Kill the umpire, he's blind as a bat!" But through the years the men in blue have stood their ground and have proven themselves worthy of their vested authority.

Tom Perryman II, a sixth grader from Dallas, Texas, has designed a machine that calls balls and strikes so accurately there just could not be any argument. The idea calls for an energized crystal beneath home plate to determine strikes and balls by computing the time it takes for sound waves to leave the crystal, strike the ball, and echo back to re-energize the crystal. The individual strike zone between shoulders and knees would be predetermined by a computer programmed for each batter. Balls on the inside or outside would not register because they would pass on either side of the waves.

But even with all this accuracy, baseball is so tied to tradition (only one major change in fifty years), we just would not get our money's worth without hearing "Play Ball" from a real ump. And anyway, who wants to argue with a mechanical ump? But maybe you could kick "him," and get away with it.

Even though fans have grumbled, "We've been robbed," only one umpire was ever actually expelled for crooked work. Richard Higham in 1882 was fired forever when it was found that he was advising gamblers how to bet on games which he called.

Surprisingly enough, the television replay has become a real friend of the umpire. The accuracy of the umpire has been shown to be excellent, particularly since baseball is a split-second game, and decisions are made instantly. All must agree, with a few exceptions, the ump has not been as blind as we once thought.

It is clear that the blind ones have really been the fans and players all these years. It is embarrassing how emotion can trick the eyes of the watching crowds.

"Eyes they have, but they see not," are paraphrased words from the Bible that could aptly describe the spectator in the stands (see Mark 8:18). Not only is this true of sporting crowds, but of people in general. And it is true concerning the spiritual workings of God. Even in this enlightened age man is still "blind as a bat."

We see and behold the moon shot on television, but we are blind to the poverty of our fellowman down the street. We see the skin of our neighbor, but are blind to the need of his heart. We see the wonders of the universe, but are blind to the hand of God. Jesus said it truthfully, "They seeing, see not."

When I went to spring training at Vero Beach, Florida, my first year off the Oklahoma University Campus, I felt I was ready for the big leagues. As a left-handed pitcher, I had a good fast ball, but a poor curve. In fact, the only kind of curve I knew was the old "round house" type that did not drop as it came toward the batter.

Jack Banta, my manager and former Dodger pitching reliever, said, "Son, you will never make it out of spring training unless you learn to make your curve ball drop down as it nears the batter." Even though Banta worked with me for days, I still could not see how to pitch the curve properly.

One day out of desperation, I came to Banta and said, "Show me again—I'll try any way you say." For the first time, I gripped the ball firmly and rolled it over my index finger and snapped my wrist as Banta had shown me. Immediately the ball rotated correctly and dropped over the plate. Suddenly my eyes flashed with understanding. Now I could see it! All the other times before, I had tried to do it *my way* and always failed. For the first time, my eyes were opened to the real curve ball, and my baseball career had new life. I would have missed three of the happiest years of my life as a professional if I had allowed myself to remain "blind as a bat."

Jesus came into this world so that men could see God in all of his fullness and love, "Whoever has seen me has seen the Father" (John 14:9, TEV). But the sad thing is that most people refuse to open their eyes to God and his leading. Even the disciples of Jesus were often "blind as bats" when it came to the real issues of life.

Time and again, Jesus told them that he was going to die on the cross for their sins, but they just could not see what he meant. It was not until after he died and arose from the grave that their eyes were opened. They were blinded because they could not see that the death of Christ on the cross actually meant life everlasting for believers. But when Jesus appeared unto them after he arose from the grave, "Their eyes were opened and they recognized him" (Luke 24:31, TEV).

Then because they could see what the cross really meant, the disciples went about telling the whole world, "That which we have seen and heard declare we unto you" (1 John 1:3, KJV).

It is sad—but true—that many look at God as if he were a spiritual umpire in black, sitting in heaven, and watching down on the activities of man. They feel that God not only judges man, but delights in calling him "out" at his slightest failure.

Because of this false idea about the nature of God, they, too, join the crowds and cry out, "Kill the umpire." There are actually people who feel the world would be a better place without God and the Bible. Like atheist advocate, Madalyn Murray O'Hare, they are out to "get" God and his Bible.

You see these people are blind to the true and living

God. He is not just sitting in the heavens laughing at his poor earthly creatures, but he lives among us. God is not just a cold, immovable judge who hates people. God is the heavenly Father who loves and cares for us. Jesus said, "Look at the birds! . . . Your heavenly Father feeds them. And you are far more valuable to him than they are" (Matt. 6:26, TLB).

Through the presence of the Holy Spirit, God is active in the world today. His supernatural power is seen by his followers.

Thomas, one of the disciples, just couldn't believe that Jesus was alive after he was crucified and buried. "I won't believe it until I see" (John 20:25, TLB), were his words. Seeing was believing for him.

Then, after eight days Jesus actually appeard in the same room with the disciples. Thomas was amazed. He could hardly believe it. But there Jesus stood.

Immediately his words of unbelief raced through his mind, "Seeing is believing." Without hesitating, Thomas fell to his knees and cried out, "My Lord and my God" (John 20:28, TLB).

Jesus said, "You believe because you have seen." And then Jesus spoke as if he were speaking to you and me. "Blessed are those who haven't seen me and believe anyway" (John 20:29, TLB).

Atheists can throw all the "cream puffs" they like at God and scream at the top of their lungs, "Kill the umpire," but they will never get rid of our loving God.

FIFTH INNING
Twin Killing

From Tinker-to-Evers-to-Chance immediately reminds the many baseball fans of one of the most fantastic double-play combinations that ever played on the diamond. Joe Tinker was the shortstop, Johnny Evers played second base, and Frank Chance held down the first base slot. This trio led the Chicago Cubs to three National League pennants and two World Series in the years 1906-1908.

The double play is the fastest play in all of baseball. From the time the ball is hit, two outs can be completed in less than five seconds. It is the strongest defensive play of the game, and baseball strategists plan hard to set it up in almost every inning when runners are on base. The team that cannot make the double play consistently cannot win the pennant. In fact, the ideal team has its own defensive strength down the middle: catcher, pitcher, centerfielder, and of course, the keystone combination of second base and shortstop.

Because of the quickness of the play, it looks rather easy, but that can only come after months of hard practice. The key is the working together of the shortstop and second baseman. These two men must be ready to move together on every pitch. They need to know each other's movements so well they can throw the ball instantly and be assured that the other man will be at the bag—ready to relay on to first base.

Timing is the important factor. These so called "Keystone Kids" throw the ball with amazing confidence and precision. When executed correctly, it is done in such a machine-like smoothness and rhythm that the crowds are stunned by its swiftness. Two outs are made in one play and thus gets the billing the "Twin Killing."

Because of the demand to work so closely together, many double-play artists soon become friends off the diamond. Often, these men room together on the road to better understand each other.

Amazingly enough, this was not true of that unbeatable double-play combination of shortstop Joe Tinker and second baseman Johnny Evers. These two great infielders who played side by side for years had a quarrel over a small matter. The argument ballooned out of proportion until it was known throughout the major leagues that this immortal double-play combination did not so much as exchange a single word. Some say that silence continued for twenty-five years!

Many baseball experts say that the double play is the most important single defensive play in baseball. The double play is looked upon as the key to the whole defense. There is a key to living life, too. Jesus Christ said that the key is found in the commandments of God.

A lawyer asked Jesus, "Which is the greatest commandment in the law?" (Matt. 22:36, TEV).

Jesus said, "you must love the Lord your God with all

your heart, and with all your soul, and with all your mind.' This is the greatest and the most important commandment. The second most important commandment is like it: 'you must love your neighbor as yourself" (Matt. 22:37-39, TEV).

And then Jesus concluded, "On these two commandments hang all the law and prophets" (Matt. 22:40, KJV). In other words, all of life hinges upon these two commandments.

I found in my many days of baseball that the most happy and satisfied ballplayers were those who put God first in their lives. These were the athletes who also were most willing to share their knowledge of the game with the younger, inexperienced players.

It is also interesting to note that success in baseball did not cause these men to become conceited and to think more of themselves than they should. It is strange, but I have almost forgotten their heroics on the field, but I shall never forget their friendliness off the field. Those who loom dearest to me are Don Demeter, Dodger outfielder, who carried the Bible in his suitcase on every road trip; Carl Erskine, whose secret pitch was faith in God; Lindy McDaniel of the Cards who had strong convictions for truth, right, and God; and Alvin Dark, who had compassion for the underdog. But probably the most unforgettable faith experience for me came from a minor league outfielder, Harvey Combs. San Jose, California, had a new, modern ball park that put the other city parks to shame. Unlike the older parks with the wooden outfield fence, San Jose had one of concrete.

In a close, tense game, a line shot was drilled to centerfield and Harvey Combs raced back to the wall in an attempt to make the game-saving catch. But just as he reached for the ball, he hit the concrete wall. Dazed and almost unconscious, he somehow managed to find the ball that had caromed off the wall. In a last-ditch effort, he threw it to the onrushing shortstop. Then like a great warrior going down in battle, he collapsed on the field. Unconscious, Combs was carried off the playing field. It was Harvey's last game, for the crash into the wall had ended his short career.

But the one thing that has stayed in my mind all these years were the words of that faithful Christian outfielder while he was in the hospital, "My life is in God's hands, whether I play baseball or not." Harvey knew the key to life: "God first."

A shortstop without the help of a second baseman could never complete the crucial double play. Jesus was saying the same thing in a spiritual way. To really love God means that you love man, too. On the other hand, to really love man you must love God as well. One without the other just will not work. The commandments of God are tied together with love for God and man.

One person so aptly pointed out that to love God is a vertical outreach toward heaven, while loving man is a horizontal outreach on earth. *The vertical love for God placed over the horizontal love for man forms a cross.*

It is the cross of Jesus Christ that has brought man to God and man to man. It is the cross of Jesus Christ that is the key to life. Jesus said, "Because I live, you also will live" (John 14:19, TEV).

Who can ever forget the story that Jesus gave us concerning the poor, beaten, dying Jew lying on the side of the road (Luke 10:30-37). Some thieves had ambushed him, attempted to kill him, stole all that he had—even the clothes that he was wearing—and left him for dead.

A religious leader came by and looked at him but offered no help. Another religious man came along a little later and walked over to see the injured man. But he, too, only *looked* at him and went on his way without lifting his finger to help the poor, half-dead man.

And then a man who wasn't a Jew at all—in fact, he was a despised half-breed called a Samaritan—came along. He, too, cautiously looked at the man in the ditch. But somehow there came a deep feeling of concern in his heart for this helpless Jew.

Even though it was a risk, he knelt down next to the man and gave him first aid with some bandages and medicine that he had brought for his own personal use. Then he placed the wounded man on his own donkey and took him to the nearest public lodging place and treated his injuries all night. The next day before the Samaritan stranger left to go about his business, he handed the innkeeper two pence, enough to take care of the man for several days and then said to the manager, "If his bill runs higher than that, I'll pay the difference the next time I am here' " (Luke 10:35, TLB). By this story Jesus was telling us that the man who really had God in his heart was the Samaritan who stopped to help his fellowman. Religion alone, all by itself, is not the key to life. True religion is the kind that causes us to help others as we go along in life. It is not always easy to love your neighbor as yourself, especially if it may cause him to get ahead of you. It is easy to help a rookie by showing him some "pro trade secrets," but it's a lot more difficult to help a seasoned pro who could take your position away from you!

Larry Hamilton was a committed Christian and an outstanding athlete. At Wichita, Kansas, North High School, he was a three-sport letterman. We all looked upon him as a superstar in all respects of the word. Larry played centerfield for our state champion baseball club. As a senior he looked like a cinch to claim that position again.

Larry, because he loved the Lord, was the kind of person who would always try to help the other guy. Fred, my twin brother, was a junior and Larry's backup man. Time and again Larry would advise his lesser competitor, Fred, and so a warm friendship developed between the two outfielders.

But it didn't take long for Coach "Monk" Edwards to realize that he had a pro prospect in his second stringer. Soon Larry, too, recognized that his centerfield position was in jeopardy by his younger trainee. But Larry Hamilton kept on teaching Fred, even with the knowledge that all his help might land him on the bench one day.

During a close game, Fred came off the bench to replace Larry in centerfield. It was a blow to the pride of any senior to be replaced by a junior. As the boys exchanged places, Larry stopped Fred and said, "Watch the runner, Charlie Gill, at first base. He will try to go all the way to third on a hit. Be ready to throw him out."

No sooner had the game again gotten under way that the next batter drove a "blue darter" over second base toward centerfield. The ball took two bounces and Fred gloved it. Looking up, he spied the speedster, Gill, heading toward third base, just as Larry had warned. Without hesitating a moment, Fred let go of the horsehide and threw it toward third. One bounce, and the ball zipped perfectly into the waiting glove of the big third sacker, Harold Dwyer. A split second later, the sliding foot of Gill hit the gloved hand of Dwyer. The runner was out! The game was over! North High had won!

From that game on, Fred stood in centerfield while Larry sat the bench.

Larry Hamilton's love for God went beyond himself to his fellowman. The words of Jesus stood out in his life, "Love thy neighbor as thyself."

SIXTH INNING
Sign Him Up

"PLAY BALL!" As these exciting words are sounded, the adrenalin begins to flow in abundance. Almost everyone likes to play on a baseball team, even when choosing up sides, and you are the last one chosen. With just a bat and ball, a handful of kids can have the time of their lives.

Some of the most enjoyable times that I can remember were those "pick up" games in a vacant lot. Any kid would do, just so we had enough for a pitcher and a couple of fielders. Even though the game we played was an imitation of the official version, the fun of competing was just as real. We would play all day with nothing stopping the game, unless the kid who owned the only bat would get mad and go home, taking his bat with him, and ending the fun.

Why, I loved the game so much that my twin and I would match up a contest with a stick and rock and go to it. And many times in the dead of the winter, with a three-inch Kansas snow on the ground, we would bundle up in coats, hats, and gloves, and play our rendition of "winter ball." Those were the days! In any vacant lot or pasture, we would swat the ball and then "motor" around the bases. No smart-aleck rules like called strikes or balls. Just hit and run!

I remember my first baseball uniform. I trembled with excitement as I stretched my legs into the pants and then walked to the mirror to see myself as a real ballplayer. The dreams of Yankee Stadium would then fill my mind as I stood in the bedroom gazing at myself in the mirror, wondering if that day would come. When does a boy become a part of his dream?

In baseball a boy has to wait awhile, but in God's work it can be right now. A boy was sitting in a crowd of 5,000 hearing Jesus preach about the kingdom of God. It was late in the evening, and everyone became hungry. There was not enough money to buy all the needed food. In the midst of the crowd, this boy came forward and offered Jesus all the food he had. It was only five fishes and two loaves, but Jesus accepted the food and prayed over it. Before their very eyes, the food was multiplied enough to feed thousands. And after all had eaten, twelve baskets of food were left over!

Not every boy has a chance to become a professional baseball player. Some, try as they may, will never make it. They need more than just a bat and a ball. But what is the stuff that makes a ballplayer? Who really knows who is good enough to play in the pros? What do baseball scouts look for in a boy as he plays the game?

Bert Wells, Brooklyn Dodger scout, had kept his eyes on my twin and me for five years. Three of those years were while we played for North Wichita High School. We won the Kansas High School championship our senior year, with Fred driving in the runs and me doing my share of the pitching. After high school, we played for the University of Oklahoma on baseball scholarships.

Then the thrilling day came! It was September 17, 1954, in our modest home in Wichita, Kansas. I sat around the old kitchen table with Fred, Mom, Dad, and Dodger scout, Bert Wells. My twin and I inked a Class "B" Dodger contract that day, and I felt ready to fly to Vero Beach, Florida, for spring training that very moment. With one swoop of the pen I had become a pro!

The baseball scout is a difficult man to understand as he goes about selecting young men to ink a contract with his club. Just what New York Yankee scout, Tom Greenwade, saw in an unknown Oklahoma high school shortstop named Mickey Mantle, no one really knew at that time. Thousands of other high school ballplayers looked the same to most people, but in that seventeen-year-old shortstop playing for the Commerce, Oklahoma, high school, Tom knew immediately he had found greatness. Mickey's play was ragged, and many baseball people held little future for the sandy-haired kid. But in the next few years, Mickey Mantle was rewriting Yankee history as a brilliant outfielder and soon became one of the greatest sluggers of all time. Mickey's 565-foot, tape-measure homer in 1953 is still considered probably the longest on record.

Have you ever wondered what Jesus saw in the twelve men he chose to follow him and become disciples? To the world they were insignificant fellows. Not one was rich or famous or influential. They were just ordinary guys like you and I. And yet Jesus staked his whole cause upon these seemingly insignificant twelve men.

Just plain men of the earth: farmers, fishermen, and small government officials. They simply heard the voice of the Lord say, "Follow me," and they left their nets and plows and tax collecting—and became disciples.

The importance of a good scout to a major league organization cannot be overestimated. The scout holds much of the future of the club in his hands. He must see more than the fans do, more than just runs, hits, and errors. He must judge actions, reflexes, intelligence, and desire. The scout goes over back roads, to villages, small towns, anywhere he might see a ball game and find another Mickey Mantle or Sandy Koufax.

Even the most alert and knowledgeable baseball men do not always recognize talent in untried hopefuls. Little Phil Rizzuto worked out at Brooklyn's Ebbets Field and was brushed aside by Casey Stengel. Soon afterwards, Phil was discovered by the Yankee's Paul Krichell and became one of the great shortstops of all time. Many other players, including some of the great ones, have similar stories to tell.

The aim of every professional baseball scouting effort is to secure the ideal team. The name of the game is to win, and that means having the very best players possible.

Through the years, there have been many super clubs who, with awesome power and speed, have hit and pitched their way to sporting fame. No one can forget the 1927 New York Yankees, "The Window Breakers," they were called. They were thought by many to be the greatest team ever assembled. Led by players like Babe Ruth, Lou Gehrig, and Bob Meusel, they soon received their second alias and were dubbed "Murderer's Row."

John McGraw's Giant clubs, which won four consecutive pennants early in the twenties, were without a doubt one of the greatest teams. Then, there was Connie Mack's Athletics who won three pennants in 1929-31. Never to be forgotten is "The Gashouse Gang," those wacky St.

Louis Cardinals of the depression year, 1934. Its colorful, flamboyant players, led by "Dizzy" Dean, "Pepper" Martin, and Manager Leo "The Lip" Durocher, personified baseball folklore.

Then, of course, the magnificent Yankee teams under zany Casey Stengel—they won ten pennants in twelve years! The year 1969 brought on the "Amazing Mets," the "rags to riches" phenomenon. Then the Oakland A's came along with three World Series victories in a row. And "The Big Red Machine," the Cincinnati Reds, were crowned world champions due to the tremendous play of men like Pete Rose, Johnny Bench, and Joe Morgan.

The disciples of Jesus were far from being called an ideal group, even in the religious world. Just a look at some of the ragged castoffs, and one would almost question the Lord's discernment. A rundown of the twelve quickly gives us doubt as to their being chosen and called.

Peter   Impulsive, braggadocio, short-tempered, and cowardly

James   Ambitious, jealous and hot tempered, always needing strength of John his brother

John   Prejudiced, jealous, inexperienced in life

Matthew   Money conscious, disloyal countryman

Thomas   Doubter, criticizer, of little faith.

Andrew   Lived in shadow of his brother, Peter— always second.

And the rest—Philip, Simon the Zealot, Nathaniel, James the son of Alphaeus, and Thaddaeus—were all so bland in personality and work that we find only traces of their names. Judas Iscariot, of course, we know as Judas the betrayer of Jesus.

Yet, all together, they teamed up to become the mightiest force in history . . . the church of Jesus Christ.

So regardless of how insignificant you may feel, God has a place for you. In Christ *the real you* can be found. "If any man be in Christ, he is a new creature; old things are passed away; and behold, all things have become new" (2 Cor. 5:17, KJV).

There wasn't a more unfit follower of Jesus than the old-time Chicago baseball outfielder, Billy Sunday. He was rag-tag all the way. Sunday was raised by his mother, because his father was killed as a soldier before he was born. So, at a very early age Billy was on his own. Soon he picked up all the vices around him, along with a vulgar-type language.

Yet, God was up to something in his life. At an early age, God opened the doors for Billy to play professional baseball with the Chicago White Sox. He was rough and tumble all the way and earned a reputation for being the fastest man in baseball, usually sliding into the bag head first.

But through all of that scrapping and kicking, God was preparing this mouthy baseballer for His work. Billy Sunday was to be a special messenger for the kingdom of God. *The Omaha Daily News* quoted Sunday's testimony in October, 1915:

> Twenty-seven years ago I walked down a street

in Chicago in company with some ball players
who were famous in this world—some of them
are dead now—and we went into a saloon. It
was Sunday afternoon and we got tanked up
and then went and sat down on a corner. I
never go by that street without thanking God
for saving me. It was a vacant lot at that time.
We sat down on a curbing. Across the street a
company of men and women were playing on
instruments—horns, flutes and slide trombones—
and the others were singing the gospel hymns
that I used to hear my mother sing back in the
log cabin in Iowa and back in the old church
where I used to go to Sunday School.

And God painted on the canvas of my recollection and memory a vivid picture of the scenes of other days and other faces.

Many have long since turned to dust. I sobbed and sobbed and a young man stepped out and said, "We are going down to the Pacific Garden Mission. Won't you come down to the mission? I am sure you will enjoy it. You can hear drunkards tell how they have been saved and girls tell how they have been saved from the red-light district."

I arose and said to the boys, "I'm through. I am going to Jesus Christ. We've come to the parting of the ways," and I turned my back on them. Some of them laughed and some of them mocked me; one of them gave me encouragement; others never said a word.

Twenty-seven years ago I turned and left that

little group on the corner of State and Madison Streets and walked to the little mission and fell on my knees and staggered out of sin and into the arms of the Saviour.!

The next day I had to get out to the ball park and practice. Every morning at ten o'clock we had to be out there. I never slept that night. I was afraid of the horse laugh that gang would give me because I had taken my stand for Jesus Christ.

I walked down to the old ball grounds. I will never forget it. I slipped my key into the wicket gate and the first man to meet me after I got inside was Mike Kelly.

Up came Mike Kelly; he said, "Bill, I'm proud of you! Religion is not my long suit, but I'll help you all I can." Up came Anson, the best ball player that ever played the game; Pfeffer, Clarkson, Flint, Jimmy McCormick, Burns, Williamson and Dalrymple. There wasn't a fellow in that gang who knocked; every fellow had a word of encouragement for me.

That was the beginning of a new life for one of the most amazing evangelists in the world. He soon gave up his illustrious baseball career to work full-time for God. Later he began holding revival meetings all over the United States.

His baseball-preaching antics brought embarrassment to the established clergy, but the crowds followed him just the same by the tens of thousands. Somehow God planned for this uncultured, fighting-type personality to bring the gospel to the man on the street. No one can ever explain former baseballer Billy Sunday's success as a preacher except in the plan of God.

"For my thoughts are not your thoughts, neither are your ways my ways, saith the Lord" (Isa. 55:8, KJV).

As one poet so aptly has written:

> I dreamed death came the other night
> And heaven's gate swung wide,
> An angel with a halo bright
> Ushered me inside.
>
> There to my astonishment
> Stood folks I'd judged and labeled,
> As quite unfit, of little worth
> And spiritually disabled.
>
> Indignant words rose to my lips,
> But never were set free,
> For every face showed stunned surprise,
> Not one expected me.

SEVENTH INNING
The Seventh Inning Stretch

Why and how the tradition of standing up before the home half of the seventh inning came about no one really knows. Some say that it happened when President Taft attended the opening day game in 1908 to throw out the first ball. The benches in that day were rough and provided hard seating, particularly for one who was not a baseball buff. Just as the Washington club was ready to bat their half of the seventh inning, President Taft stood to relax his 300-pound, body. At the sight of seeing the president on his feet, thousands of spectators in the stands also stood to get a glimpse of the president—until the entire crowd was upon its feet and craning its necks to see him. So it was that "the seventh inning stretch" was born—and it has even survived the luxurious, comfortable seats of stadia like the Astrodome.

Baseball just wouldn't be the same without its peculiar traditions and fans. The fans that go through the turnstiles make up the crowd that roars with excitement. And the roar that is often heard in the stands isn't just a rumbling noise, either—it's a language! It speaks, not only to the spectator, but pours out onto the playing field and actually influences the game. Every real fan in the stands and every ballplayer on the field feel its vibrations and respond to its call.

The seventh inning stretch is the time to stand up between innings and give your hometown team full support. Today is the time for believers to stand up and be counted for the sake of Christ. Too long we have been lost in the noisy crowd. Too long we have allowed the world to choke out our witness about Jesus. Too long we have sat watching instead of rising to the occasion to let the world know we believe in God.

Nothing inspires a team more than seeing its rooters rise in mass and in one great voice boom out encouragement.

Most seasoned ballplayers tune down that roar, but none can tune it out entirely. Even one of the most competitive, bloodthirsty ballplayer of them all, Leo "The Lip" Durocher, once quipped, "I cannot play to empty benches."

It is the crowd that makes baseball more than a sporting pleasure. Fans who rightly get their tagged name from the word *fanatic* are as much of baseball as the ball and bat. The fan by his actions and devotion to the game has made it become sort of a religion.

Sports have become such an allurement that many worship their idols on the field of competition. Some have actually become so captivated by the game, it has become their one consuming devotion in life.

For some, going to the baseball stadium has replaced going to church, pulling for the home team has replaced prayer, reading the sports page has replaced the Bible, the thrill of the home runs has replaced the excitement of seeing a person come to God, the winning of the World Series has replaced the joy of looking toward heaven.

Some fans have become so wrapped up in the game that

on occasions they have spilled out onto the diamond, riots have occurred, causing injuries to player and spectator alike.

In 1940, Detroit came to Cleveland to meet the Indians. The Tigers had called the Cleveland club "cry babies," among other names, so the Cleveland fans were ready with indignation. As the game got under way, there was an almost constant shower of eggs, fruits, and vegetables from the stands. But the vegetable cloudburst came to a sudden halt when "Birdie" Tebbetts, Detroit catcher, was knocked unconscious by a bushel basket full of tomatoes, thrown from the upper stands.

Now, the missle-throwing crowds have been curtailed in most cities by guards who stand at the turnstiles and confiscate potential projectiles such as bottles, cans, and vegetable "grenades." But unfortunately, a few still manage to smuggle in their arsenal to throw their vengeance onto the field of play. This fanaticism can sweep across an entire stadium crowd like a prairie fire.

Crowds have always had their influence upon man and history. But it is more than interesting that the crowds who followed Jesus did not influence his ultimate purpose. The Bible states that, "He steadfastly set his face to go to Jerusalem" (Luke 9:51, KJV), even though it meant certain death. Certainly it was the mob who killed him, but ironically enough, that was why he came to earth. It is amazing that the foolish crowd never realized that Jesus went to the cross for them.

In all of baseball there was no crowd like the Brooklyn Dodger fans from "Flatbush." They had a mania for their "Bums" that is indescribable. The explosion of excitement from the stands in so-called "Brooklynese" still rings in the now silent Dodger Stadium, old Ebbetts Field.

"T'row it down his t'roat" and "wait'l next year," could only come from the heart and lungs of the Bedford Avenue crowd. The screaming warhoops and ringing cowbells finally gave Brooklyn its first World Series in 1955. The Dodgers had come of age that year and earned respectability for the "Bums." Walter Alston, manager, and Walter O'Malley, owner, were heralded as men of the century. But the garb of respectability soon became the downfall for the fans. For old Ebbetts Field with its deteriorating surroundings could no longer be a home for the "new Dodgers." In three years, the "Bums" had found greener pastures across the continent in Los Angeles.

It was a stinging blow to baseball's greatest fans, but fans are always emotional and too often are unaware of the true facts behind the sporting scene. When the big move by the Dodgers became publicly known, President Walter O'Malley was despised by the once loyal crowds throughout the five boroughs. They had forgotten that O'Malley, a native Brooklynite himself, had worked hard for years to build a better stadium to keep the Dodgers in Brooklyn.

But the fans "blew their tops" and labeled O'Malley a "traitor" and an "ingrate." City Hall issued condemning statements, and the City Council passed resolutions. Politicians made broad promises to keep the Dodgers in town. But the fact still remained that a new stadium and facilities were not built, giving the team no other choice but to relocate. Baseball is better off because of the move, but some fans will never get over it.

For the most part, the crowds that followed Jesus also were emotional and unaware of the true facts. Jesus knew this and that is why, even though he loved them, he never let them sway him from his mission to save them from their sins.

At first, they called him a great teacher for they were "astonished at his doctrine" (Luke 4:32, KJV). As the crowds began to grow, Jesus performed miracles to show them that God was in their midst. These miracles made him so popular and sought after that he literally had to hide from them to get even a few hours of privacy.

The crowds began to call him "one sent from God," because of his work. Some began seeing the makings of a ruler, even a king. This is just what the little country of Palestine needed to break away from Roman government rule. "Let's make him our king," came the joyous cry. "Hosanna in the highest," was heard in the streets of Jerusalem and Jesus was almost mobbed by the crowd, which would have forced him to accept the crown.

But Jesus knew that his work was to build the kingdom of God. So, he disappeared just at the moment the crowds were ready to acclaim him their earthly king.

Then the roar began to be heard in the crowd, "Who said he was a teacher of truth? Why, he is a liar, he said he could tear down the Temple and in three days rebuild it!"

"A miracle worker from God, you say? Oh, he works miracles alright, but it is by the power of the devil," came another remark from the jeering crowd.

"And call him a king, would you! He eats with just the common sinners of the streets. The only crown he needs is one of thorns, and the throne he should possess is the cross. Crucify him! Crucify him!"

But not all of the people in the crowd are demanding

and fickle. There are some who are not swayed by the emotion and disappointment of the moment. A real commitment that continues year in and year out is found among a few.

My Aunt Mary was a baseball fan like that. Day in and day out she would sit by the old radio cabinet, all the while rocking back and forth, intently listening to the account of her hapless Pittsburg Pirates. This was during the depression days of the thirties, so it was not unusual to have several families occupying one large house. Such was the case of the Minton family. Then, with money being scarce or in some cases nonexistent, the Mintons had an inexpensive brand of recreation. In a normal afternoon twenty or more of all ages, from grandpa on down to the smallest grandchild, huddled around the "family entertainment center," the large console radio, listening to the baseball game.

From inning to inning the little crowd in the living room would change in size and faces. But always faithful to the ninth inning, Aunt Mary would sit and listen.

"Aunt Mary," I would ask, "Why do you like the Pittsburg Pirates? They have been in the cellar for years!"

"I don't know," would come her Oklahoma-drawled answer, "but I've been a'followin' them for thirty years, ever since they won the World Series in 1909."

"Have you ever lived in Pittsburg?"

"No," she replied, "I've never even seen that big city. Why, I haven't ever seen the Pirates play, for that matter."

"But—Aunt," I implored, "don't you know they are in last place without a chance to win?"

"Sure do," came her answer with a tiny smile, "but next year may be their year!" Aunt Mary had to wait twenty-one more years until 1960! That year Bill Mazeroski, leading off the ninth inning in the seventh game of the World Series, clubbed a home run to beat the Yankees. But all of her waiting had been worthwhile. Aunt Mary was a baseball fan.

Almost every big league park has a "pet" fan who becomes a part of its personality and tradition. How it happens no one really knows. The Dodgers in Ebbetts Field will always remember the cowbell-ringing Hilda Chester. The Polo Grounds' devoted early-day fan was Frank H. Wood, who would stand and scream, "Well! Well!" The Boston Red Sox fans were led by a saloon keeper who called his gang, "Royal Rooters." And recently the Chicago Cubs in Wrigley Field have a college-age group which call itself "Bleacher Bums."

Years ago, fans in Chicago discovered the joy of organized rooting, stamping, and clapping in unison to distract the pitcher. They also shouted out such requests as "take him out!" in loud rhythm. It nearly shook the rafters. Ban Johnson, then baseball commissioner, was determined to stop it, or as he thought, "It would grow into proportions past control and would soon bring baseball into disrepute."

But Ban Johnson could no more stop organized rooting than he could have had all the fans removed. Soon every city had its formal or informal organized rooters.

The electricity of enthusiasm and excitement that races through a crowd, and then a city, when the pennant is at stake cannot be contained. It is an involvement beyond control. But, baseball is built upon winners, and when a team begins to lose, you can hardly give the tickets away. The excitement melts into disappointing frustration, and slowly the stadium becomes an empty corpse.

The crowds who followed Jesus soon began to realize that he would not be their championed leader. He talked too much about spiritual things, instead of the things of the world. One by one they left him, until at one time only his close disciples may have remained.

Looking at his now-lonely disciples, Jesus asked, "Will you also go away?" (John 6:67, RSV). Simon Peter, speaking for that small, faithful band and reflecting their true commitment, said, "Lord, to whom shall we go? You have the words of eternal life!" (John 6:68, RSV).

As we live among the crowds today, the words of Simon Peter speak for us, too.

EIGHTH INNING
The Sermon on the Mound

I was riding the crest of a six-game winning streak when our Dodgers faced the Giant farm club of Muskogee, Oklahoma. There was not a trace of a thought of losing in my mind. I strode out to the mound not only confident, but almost carelessly cocky. That night I was ready to burn the ball past them and rack up number seven in a row. It was my rookie year, and that night was going to show me that I had a lot to learn about the pros.

The first inning seemed like a nightmare. Everything I threw to the plate exploded on their bats like TNT. Before I could get my bearings, the score was 3 to 0, with two men on base and no outs. I just could not believe it!

My twin brother, Fred, was playing centerfield for us, and what a "ball hawk" he was. When I was on the mound, I knew that if anyone could make the impossible catch, he would. Twice that night he hit the wall going after the long drives. But the way Muskogee was hitting, no one, not even Fred, could "flag" the ball down.

Jack Banta, my manager, finally made his way to the mound to rescue his bewildered rookie. But I felt good. My fast ball seemed to move, and so I confidently said to Banta, "Let me stay and pitch to one more. I'm loose now, and I'll get the side out."

Banta hesitated, and while he was thinking, a voice came booming in towards the mound. It was my poor, bedraggled twin brother, Fred. He was leaning up against the old, green wooden fence in centerfield. He was yelling at the top of his lungs, "Take the bum out! He's killing me!"

With those words of desperation, Banta took one look at me and said, "How can I argue with that?" And with no further conversation, I headed for the showers.

It is never fun to lose; winning has always been in my blood. But life doesn't give us a good bounce everyday. Some people get bitter in defeat and become mad at God and the world.

But I have found that even in defeat, God walks with true Christians. As I walked defeatedly from the mound, past the white-chalked third base line, on into the dugout, into the clubhouse, and finally to the showers as a loser, *I knew I was a winner.* The game was lost, but my life was a winner. Why? Because I possessed something that even baseball could not give. When I was eleven years of age, I gave my life to Jesus Christ, and I found in him the victory. I have lost a lot of games, but I will never be a loser, because Jesus is my Savior.

In a strange, unexplainable way, the game looks different from the mound. The batters are bigger and meaner. Their bats become war clubs. The strike zone shrinks to a pinpoint. Home plate is a small, white rubber dot. The sixty feet, six-inch distance from the mound to the plate is a mile. The spaces between the outfielders enlarge to Texas-sized ranches. The fences creep in just behind second base. The ump suddenly turns into a Mafia figure.

The fans breathe down your neck. The pressure that goes with being a pitcher on the mound distorts everything.

This strange, pressurized feeling is felt more by the pitcher than any other player, because he is the one most responsible for the outcome of the game. Within the grasp of his hand is that five ounce sphere of horsehide and string that controls the game. Pitching is 70 to 90 percent of baseball. The team that has the best pitching is the team that wins the pennant.

This is why the pitcher is usually the highest paid ballplayer on the field. Pitcher Jim "Catfish" Hunter is being paid $3.7 million by the New York Yankees over the five-year period of 1975-80. It is believed to be the most expensive contract in the history of professional sports.

But there is more to the thrill of pitching than money. Every play is centered around the mound, and every eye watches every move. The pitcher is the key man.

Since the 1890's, pitchers have commanded top headlines. In fact, pitchers have become so proficient that many experts have predicted they would ruin the game. As far back as 1893, some baseball owners thought that the new "cyclone"-type pitcher would deaden the game. They thought the public wanted to see more slugging, and the batter seemed almost paralyzed by the new scientific pitcher. As curve balls became sharper and more difficult to hit, suggestions such as allowing pitchers to throw only fast balls, the introduction of a "live" ball, and ordering stationary zones made their way into baseball executives' discussions. But none of these tactics became part of the rules.

To bring even more science into the early game, Professor Hinton of Harvard invented the first mechanical pitching machine. The machine was like a cannon, and it had to be set off with a powder charge. Even though it was quite accurate and could "pitch" curve, drop, and rise balls with adjusted speeds, the boom so unnerved the batsman, it was looked upon as a novelty.

The pitcher continued to dominate the game during the pre-Ruth days. Shutouts and one-run wins were standard with the bunt, hit-and-run, and the squeeze play being the rules instead of the exceptions. But Babe Ruth changed the pitchers' world. The long-ball hitting syle had come to stay, and pitching for some became a nightmare. The complete domination of the game by the pitcher had come to an end.

But even with the hitters' new golden age, the pitchers were still around to capture the lion's share of the glory. Pitchers like Walter Johnson, Carl Hubbell, Grover Cleveland Alexander, Bob Feller, and Sandy Koufax continued to keep the baseball action centered on the mound. In my opinion, Koufax was the greatest of them all.

In 1969 Sandy Koufax was voted the most outstanding athlete of the decade. His prowess as a pitcher was so great that it overshadowed the personal feats of every other athlete in all sports. A most remarkable feat for a man who found it hard to achieve success, or for that matter, even to make the team.

I remember seeing Sandy in the Dodger spring training camp in 1955. That year both of us had signed contracts with the organization as left-handed pitchers. I was destined to be a minor leaguer, because I did not possess that God-given super talent, but Sandy Koufax had it. But even with all that talent, he was one of the wildest pitchers in camp. Once I saw him pitch the ball completely over the backstop! But regardless of how wild he was, he always threw with overpowering speed.

Dodger Manager Walter Alston once remarked, "We play Sandy only when we don't have anyone else, and when I say anyone, I mean just that." So, Sandy sat the bench for six years before his greatness was really shown. Those years were full of frustration and hard work. The more frustrated he became, the harder he threw—and the harder he threw, the wilder he got. Some wondered if he would ever acquire a sense of direction.

Dodger Pitching Coach Joe Becker began to instruct Sandy. Slowly Sandy's control came, and his curve began to break with fantastic speed and accuracy. Coach Becker was able to put the kind of rhythm into Sandy's delivery that made him the superstar par excellence. Koufax's unprecedented record of having led the league in earned run average for four years in succession, pitching four no-hitters in a period from 1962-1964, and a perfect game in 1965 without question makes him the greatest pitcher who ever lived. At least that's how I feel.

Even though my talent could not be compared to Sandy's in any measure, I still recognized that what I did possess was God-given. My determination and desire was second to none. I had always loved baseball, and baseball to me meant pitching.

Somehow, there was always that pull to the mound. Whenever a group would form a pickup game, I would find myself in the middle of the diamond with the ball in my hand.

I have always had a certain fascination for pitching. That little extra excitement of being on the mound would race through my veins and make all the responsibility that went with the position worth it all. For me, pitching was the name of the game.

I had pitched two years of minor league baseball with the Dodgers and was half way through my third year when somehow, someway, God began to speak to my heart once again about preaching his Word. As a boy, I had felt this impression, but it had faded away when college and professional baseball became my passion.

At this point in my professional career, I had done reasonably well with an overall record of 35 wins and 13 losses. But somehow—in a strange way—when I stepped on that familiar mound that July evening and looked at the crowd in the stands, I did not see baseball fans anymore. I saw people on their way to hell.

I could feel the love of God pressing upon my heart, and his call became clear to me. He wanted me to preach. I knew then and there, that night on the mound, that the 1957 season would be my last as a Dodger minor leaguer. My dreams of stardom had come to an end. Now it was the kingdom of God for me, instead of the kingdom of baseball. My thoughts were now for the souls of men. I had actually "lost" my life, only to "find" it once again in a new and exciting way. What a wonderful, silent Sermon on the Mound God gave me that night at the park in Reno, Nevada.

When the new contract time came in late January, I got that desire again to try it one more season. But, I remembered that sermon on the mound in Reno. Turning down spring training in Vero Beach and the thrill of facing another batter set up a struggle within. The call of God continued to sound clear in my heart, and with the same determination I used on the mound, I reached for the higher calling. I traded my pitcher's glove for a preacher's Bible. And did you know, it was sort of like trading a diamond for a crown!

The years have flown by, and baseball for me has become only a companion of the past. For almost twenty years I have been preaching the gospel as a Southern Baptist preacher, and I can say with all sincerity I have never really looked back. But I must admit that every springtime about March, I get that little bug called "spring training fever" and glance over my shoulder to see what my Dodgers are up to for the season.

It has always given me a little added determination when I read the apostle Paul's words of encouragement:

> Brethren, I count not myself to have apprehended: but this one thing I do, forgetting those things which are behind, and reaching forth unto those things which are before, I press toward the mark for the prize of the high calling of God in Christ Jesus (Phil. 3:13-14, KJV).

With that I wholeheartedly agree, "Me too, Paul, I press on."

NINTH INNING
Don't Die on Third

A ballplayer actually died on third base during a baseball game, according to Mac Davis in his book, *Sports Shorts*. That astonishing occurrence took place around the turn of the century. Two *outstanding* semi-pro teams from Minnesota had won the attention of the baseball world. When these two teams met, one from Wilmar and one from Benson, fans came from hundreds of miles to witness the battle.

For nine innings, they played to a deadlock. Neither team was able to make the winning run. In the first half of the tenth, the Benson club scored a run. The Wilmar team then came to bat. With Theilman, the Wilmar pitcher, on first base, O'Toole smashed a terrific drive into the outfield. It looked like a sure home run, but Theilman, who was running in front of O'Toole, rounded third base and then suddenly collapsed. O'Toole passed third base a few steps behind. Unable to pass him, O'Toole picked him up and carried him, throwing Theilman across home plate ahead of him and, thus, winning the game.

Not until then was it determined that Theilman had died of a heart attack at third base!

It is amazing, but sadly true that many are dying on the third base of life. They have everything that the world can offer but are unable to really live. When Jesus Christ was here on earth, he met a man standing on the third base of life. He was young, rich, and popular. It seemed that he had everything going for him. If any man deserved to be a winner in life, it was this man. Yet his life was incomplete, and he knew it. So he came running to Jesus and asked, "Good Teacher, what must I do to inherit eternal life?" (Mark 10:17, RSV). He knew that without eternal life he was dying on the third base of life.

The Bible tells us that Jesus loved this unusually gifted young man. Jesus knew that the man was sincere and wanted to do what was right and best. Speaking straight to his heart, Jesus said, "You lack one thing; go, sell what you have, and give to the poor . . . and come, follow me" (Mark 10:21, RSV).

But the victory words of the Savior were too much for him. The Bible records the tragic scene.

"And he went away sorrowful; for he had great possessions" (Mark 10:22, RSV). The rich young man, so close to the greatest victory of life, died spiritually at third base that day.

It is disappointing to lose a game and especially with a runner on third base. Leon "Red" Ames hurled a no-hit no-run, game on the opening day of the 1909 baseball season, but he did not win the game as his New York Giants failed to get a run, so the game was lost in the thirteenth inning—1 to 0.

Baseball becomes really exciting when a runner is on third base. It is a time when every fan is sitting on the edge of his seat. The slightest bobble of the ball or misthrow may give the chance for the runner to streak home with the score.

Probably the most dangerous runner at third base was the late Jackie Robinson of the Brooklyn Dodgers. His daring base thefts on the diamond made him one of the most feared runners in the game.

My first year as a pro was Robinson's next-to-last year as an active player. Jackie's career was almost behind him then, and what a brilliant performer he had been! In 1947 as the first black man to play in major league baseball, he was voted "Rookie of the Year." Two years later, he was voted the National League's "Most Valuable Player," and that year he also won the batting championship. After leading the Dodgers into the World Series three times, and regularly being a National League All-Star, he was enshrined in the Hall of Fame.

Spring training was in full swing. That lazy, sunny afternoon in Florida brought the St. Louis Cardinals to Vero Beach. Jackie was in the starting lineup, playing at third base. Beneath his ball cap you could see the gray hair of his side burns, causing him to look more like a distinguished doctor or lawyer than a ball player. But he still commanded the respect of every player on both teams, as he stepped onto the field that March day in 1955. Without a doubt he was the elder statesman and the club leader.

As I watched the exhibition game between the Cards and the Dodgers, the score was tied in the bottom half of the ninth inning. Jackie hit a stand-up triple off the great Cardinal reliever, Lindy McDaniel. Robinson then showed that famous, daring baserunning that made him so feared by opposing teams. Up and down the third base line he ran with quick starts and stops, sometimes coming to a complete standstill as if he were begging Lindy to attempt to throw him out.

The cool, calm, and collected McDaniel seemed to ignore completely Robinson's daring antics and concentrated on pitching to the next hitter.

Suddenly, before anyone could realize what was happening, Jackie Robinson made an explosive lunge toward home plate. Immediately, McDaniel made a hurried throw to his catcher. But McDaniel's quick action was not fast enough to catch the speeding Robinson. In ahead of the throw, Jackie slid to score the winning run! It was one of the most breathtaking scenes that baseball ever afforded me! That steal of home by Jackie was just the warm up of what he was to mean to the Dodgers that year. He was the spark, even with a bad leg, that took the slumping Dodgers into the 1955 World Series to become World Champions.

Jackie's slogan on and off the field was always, "Don't die on third." That is what made him the dominant figure and the team's most aggressive ball player.

Third base is so close, only ninety feet away, and yet so far away from home plate. No game was ever won at third base; it takes home plate to give the win.

There is another young man in the Bible who was also standing on the third base of life. His position was nearly the opposite of the rich young ruler we read about earlier. Here was a person who deserved to "die on third." He came from a good home. He was loved by his family, but he wanted to live life his way, whether it was right or wrong. So, he took all of his inheritance and left home to really "live it up." And live it up he did! But when his money ran out, so did his friends.

"And not many days after the younger son gathered all together, and took his journey into a far country, and there wasted his substance with riotous living. And when he had spent all, there arose a mighty famine in that land; and he began to be in want" (Luke 15:13, 14, KJV).

The Bible tells us that this young man was determined that he was not going to die on the third base of life.

"And he went and joined himself to a citizen of that country; and he sent him into his fields to feed swine. And he would fain have filled his belly with the husks that the swine did eat: and no man gave unto him. And when he came to himself, he said, How many hired servants of my father's have bread enough and to spare, and I perish with hunger! I will arise and go to my father, and will say unto him, Father, I have sinned against heaven, and before thee, and am no more worthy to be called thy son: make me as one of thy hired servants" (Luke 15:15-19).

What a victory it was for that once-dying young man. Jesus said, "While he was still a long distance away, his father saw him coming, and was filled with loving pity and ran and embraced him and kissed him" (Luke 15:20, TLB). A royal welcome was his: the best robe was given him, the ring of the family was placed on his finger, and a feast with music was given in his honor. He was not deserving of all this—he should have "died on third," but he found at home forgiveness and a new life.

Isn't it surprising that the rich young ruler, who seemingly deserved the triumph of heaven, went away sad, while the pigpen prodigal son, who deserved to starve to death, went home to victory. God's grace is so amazing!

The forgiveness of God through Jesus Christ is the "hallmark" of the New Testament. That is why Jesus came to die on the cross. No longer do we have to die on third in the pigpen of life. We can come home to Jesus now. We could try to wait until we clean ourselves up. That would take too long, and we would certainly starve to death. We must come as we are, but do it now!

The Bible says today is the day of salvation. Life is short—we have no guarantee how long we will live.

Jesus said, "Follow me." Those words are emphatic. They mean, don't wait for anything. Come immediately, right now.

My twin brother, Fred, wrote this poem during his second year of baseball, while playing centerfield for the Baltimore Orioles' Paris, Texas, club in 1956.

On the Third Base of Life
Without A Score

> The bat was swung
> The ball was met
> He ran toward first
> He had a hit.
>
> He rejoiced inside
> As he reached the base,
> The game wasn't lost—
> "We're still in the race."
>
> Eagerly he eyed
> That second base;
> With a burst of speed,
> Slid on his face.

"Safe" yelled the ump.
The roar of the crowd
Made the player feel good,
And mighty proud!

Slapping the dust from
His uniform,
He thought to himself,
There is one more.

Ready and tense,
He must get to third,
The coach gave a sign,
He had given the word.

The pitcher wound up
And let the ball fly,
And going to third,
It was now do or die.

Dust and dirt and
An impact of cleats—
He was fightin' for third,
There were no retreats.

"Safe" yelled the ump
To the amazement of all,
For the man guarding third
Had dropped the ball.

Third base was conquered,
And it was for real.
What a great accomplishment
And such a great thrill!

A sigh of relief,
A smile on his face,
He was happy with joy—
He was standin' on base.

As a light turned out
In the dark of night,
So came the finish
Of shocking sight.

For the player forgot
About the base ahead.
"Third base doesn't count"
The score keeper said.

The player understood
That home was one more,
For he was standin' on third
Without a score.

So, when you're at bat,
And you get a hit,
Remember on third,
You've not scored yet.

For only at home
Can the Score Keeper say,
"A run has been counted—
"He came all the way."

Home by God's grace,
With Christ evermore,
And not on third base
Without faith's score.

TENTH INNING
Extra Innings

A baseball game really gets exciting when extra innings are played. One good thing about baseball is that some team must win. Every game must have a verdict.

A tie game is unheard of in baseball. "Lippy the Lip" Durocher once quipped, "A tie game is like kissing your kid sister." Baseball is so designed that an even score must be broken.

It is the extra-inning game that really gives the fan his money's worth. Every move in extra innings is important. Each pitch from the mound could be the last one. Every muscle is taut with tension.

Most baseball players agree that more energy is used in just one extra inning than the previous nine innings put together. The measure of a team's greatness usually can be weighed in the outcome of those extra-inning games.

The longest extra-inning contest on record went 26 innings between the Brooklyn Dodgers and the Boston Braves, played at Boston on May 1, 1920. Games have been deadlocked so long that some cities' curfews have caused these contests to be continued the next day. In fact, the longest extra-inning game on record was played between San Francisco and New York on May 31, 1964.

It took the Giants seven hours and twenty-three minutes to subdue the last-place Mets!

Oftentimes the Christian also experiences "extra innings" in his life. Jesus said, "If one forces you to go one mile, go with him two miles" (Matt. 5:41, RSV). The inference here is attitude, too. As you go even the first mile, don't be bitter and give obvious resentment. Then give that unexpected effort and cheerfully go the second mile.

Every manager attempts to build this kind of team spirit. Each player, even though assigned to a specific position, learns to play the other man's position. Often a pitcher must cover up first base or home plate to help his teammate.

During a Class C Pioneer League game at Great Falls, Montana, I was on the mound against the Salt Lake City club. With runners at first and third, I let go a wild pitch that sent my catcher, John Stamen, chasing the ball toward the grandstands. The runner at third was charging home like a bull. Without hesitating, I ran toward home plate just in time to catch the perfect "strike" from Stamen. With one swipe of the glove, I tagged the sliding runner out, and then looking up spied the runner at first fifteen feet off the bag.

Why the runner at first hadn't gone to second will always be a mystery (probably a scared rookie), but in an instant I relayed the ball to first base. Andy Vanderville, our huge first baseman who had charged in toward home plate, was out of play, but backing him up to take my throw was Al Norris, our second sacker, who easily put the tag on the unsuspecting runner. In each case it was the "second mile" effort that paid off.

The practice at spring training had come to fruition. Hour after hour in the early weeks of the spring at Vero Beach, Florida, we had practiced hard to make teamwork our second nature. So, when the pressure was on, we were able to perform as pros.

Every day a quiet time with God provides the training and spiritual strength for a "second mile" endurance. Each day read the Bible and pray. These simple acts of faith bring great spiritual strength into our lives. Jesus said, "If ye have faith as a grain of mustard seed, ye shall say unto this mountain, Remove hence to yonder place; and it shall remove: and nothing shall be impossible unto you" (Matt. 17:20, KJV).

I never did pray to win. To me winning or losing a baseball game is not a worthy spiritual request. I remember one game, though, when I needed that little bit "extra" to win. Again our Great Falls, Montana, club was facing Salt Lake City for the second game of a double header. I had pitched and won the first game, 3 to 0. In the ninth inning of the second game, Chuck Page had gotten tired, so off the bench I came to relieve him—with one out and runners on first and third. We were ahead, 3 to 1.

I was more than a little nervous, which caused me to walk the first batter and load the bases. The next batter hit a weak infield pop to shortstop Wayne Wiley. That made two outs.

Now the pressure was mounting: bases loaded, two outs, ninth inning! Over the public address system came the announcement I was fearing, "Now batting, Eddie Moskus." This hulk of a man had just come down to the lower minors from the AAA American Association. Eddie was a home run hitter deluxe. As he strode to the plate,

I knew I had my work cut out for me.

As if each pitch were destined to bring a storybook ending, I found myself with a full count: three balls and two strikes. One good pitch, and Moskus would knock it out of the park. One bad pitch, and I'd walk in a run and be faced with worse trouble.

Twice more I threw my best pitch, but each time Moskus' bat smashed the ball into foul territory. That "second mile" had come. With pressure at every base, the moment of truth was immediate.

With a deep breath, I turned to look toward the outfield. That moment on the mound I prayed. It was just for a second. I didn't pray to win. I didn't pray against Moskus. I prayed for strength to do my best. That would be good enough-win or lose.

Quickly turning around I got the sign from Stamen, my catcher, and rared back to give the fast ball all I ever had. Moskus was ready. Right into his strength came the ball. Swing went the bat, but somehow, some way, he missed it! The game was over—we had won!

"Second mile" efforts don't come easily, not on the baseball field or in our spiritual lives. They don't just happen. It takes heart and courage in baseball, and it takes the Holy Spirit of God in everyday life.

A minor league first baseman had an excellent fielding record. In fact, it was the best in all professional baseball for a number of years. But every year he was passed over by the big leagues for seemingly lesser players. This first baseman would not give the extra effort to field a ball. He was so careful not to make an error and spoil his record that he sometimes would cause his team to lose by not attempting to field a difficult play.

He was a "fancydan" player who looked good on the diamond. But he would never give that little extra effort when the chips were down. He simply wouldn't go that second mile to win.

There was no team like the rag-tag New York Mets club who expanded the National League in 1961 under the invincible manager, Casey Stengel. They were the clowns of the baseball world. The Mets made more errors and lost more games than any team in history. Even Casey would joke over the worst team that ever played National League baseball, "I've got to humor these guys to keep them active."

But Stengel continued to manage his cellar-ridden team and to build within them the desire to go the second mile. They were accustomed to losing; it became their way of life. But they never gave up.

Don Demeter, outfielder for the Dodgers, said, "In my book they are the toughest to play. Sure we beat them all the time, but they play as hard when they are losing as when they are winning."

The Mets just didn't know the difference whether they were winning or not. They went out to go the second mile every inning, regardless of the score or how many errors they were committing.

The wacky Mets made the grand old game of baseball almost laughable. In 1965 against Cincinnati, eighteen of them struck out and didn't get a hit in the first ten innings. Yet they beat the Reds, 1-0, on a homer by Johnny Lewis in the eleventh to end another ten-game losing streak.

Even though Casey Stengel didn't give the Mets a winner, he didn't fail, for he left them a legacy of his own spirit. Gil Hodges picked up the "second mile" spirit, and eight years after the Mets had entered big league baseball, he managed the impossible. The "second mile" amazing Mets won the 1969 National League pennant and the World Series! They simply never gave up. They were willing to pay the price to become champions.

Jesus said, "Follow me." Many seem willing, but few will go the second mile.

"And it came to pass, that, as they went in the way, a certain man said unto him, 'Lord, I will follow thee whithersoever thou goest. And Jesus said unto him, 'Foxes have holes, and birds of the air have nests; but the Son of man hath not where to lay his head.' And he said unto another, 'Follow me.' But he said, Lord, suffer me first to go and bury my father. Jesus said unto him, Let the dead bury their dead: but go thou and preach the kingdom of God. And another also said, Lord, I will follow thee; but let me first go bid them farewell, which are at home at my house. And Jesus said unto him, No man, having put his hand to the plow, and looking back, is fit for the kingdom of God" (Luke 9:57-62).

Don Demeter had one year of major league ball under his belt. He was playing behind big Duke Snider in centerfield for the Dodgers. Even though he had managed to make the club, his future with the majors had not been insured as yet.

During the off-season, Walter Alston had invited Don to play winter ball in Mexico. It was a good chance for Don to improve his long ball hitting and to try to cut down on his strikeouts.

Don, a Southern Baptist, always packed his Bible on every road trip. Each day he spent time in prayer and Bible study. "I always wanted my baseball to speak for the Lord, too," he often told reporters.

It was the eleventh inning of a tough game. The team had been on the road for several weeks and had grown tired of moving from hotel to hotel. As the game continued to drag on, Don came up to bat. Then came a request from the usually quiet Alston, "Hey, Don, hit one out of here, and get it over for us."

Demeter had never before received such a confident word from his manager. More than at any time in his life, he wanted to go "the second mile" for Alston.

Don said, "I didn't believe in just asking God to let me hit a home run. I felt I should do what I could, so I prayed, "Lord, let the pitcher throw it 'high and tight.'

"I could hardly believe my eyes," recalls Don, "for the first pitch was coming right in my strength, a fast ball, 'high and inside.' It was labeled a home run all the way! From the sound of my bat when it hit the ball, I knew it was out of the park.

"I went around the bases," continued Don. "I touched each one and said aloud, 'Thank you Lord.'

"Approaching home plate, I saw my teammates gathered to give me a hero's welcome.

"I didn't care what they thought about my 'thank you, Lord' words. With both feet, I jumped on the plate and hollered aloud for all to hear, 'Praise God!'"

What does it take to become a champion All-Star baseball player? Johnny Bench, All-Star National League catcher for the Cincinnati Reds, was interviewed recently during a Saturday baseball game telecast.

"Down at Binger, Oklahoma, I had to learn to play all the positions. You see, I was the fourth string catcher, and if I played any, it had to be somewhere else. So I patrolled the outfield and eventually worked my way to third base.

"One game in high school I came off the bench to hit a two-run home run to win the game 3 to 2, only to sit the bench the next game because I was then only the second-string catcher. But it was OK.

"Then the coach needed me to pitch so I wound up pitching. I won 16 and lost 1. We all were willing to play anywhere for the team."

To follow Jesus means that "second mile" living. In fact, it means more than that—it means your very life.

"For whosoever will save his life shall lose it: but whosoever will lose his life for my sake, the same shall save it" (Luke 9:24).

LAST INNING
After Twenty Years

After twenty years, what does an unknown baseball career mean to anyone? Probably not much except a little personal satisfaction.

Certainly, it wasn't a career of which to do much boasting. No name was ever registered in the big leagues by the name of Frank Minton. In fact, my professional career of three years barely touched the hem of the garment of baseball, but all the same it was pro ball. Most of the players never made the big time in the majors, but I did compete against or played on the same team with Don Demeter, Vada Pinson, Charlie Smith, Ed Racow, to name a few.

But what do those three years mean as I look back today? With such an unknown past, surely it had to be more than runs, hits, and errors. Now God was plenty good to me on the field as I registered, as a left-handed pitcher, 39 wins and 20 losses. But the real essence of it all was not just baseball itself.

One of my greatest joys came when I could tell the "knothole gangs" my testimony about Jesus. I remember in Great Falls, Montana, a little boy leaned over the grandstand and asked for my autograph. I signed my name on his paper and as usual wrote under my signature, ROM. 1:16.

The next evening during the pre-game warmups, as I was over near the same grandstand area and playing a game of "pepper," the same kid leaned out of the stands and said, "Me and my dad figured out that ROM. 1:16."

"Oh yeah," I curiously commented.

With much authority, the boy enthusiastically said, "R means run. O is out and M stands for Minton. The 1:16 is your pitching earned run average."

Right then and there I shared with him my favorite Bible verse, Romans 1:16: "For I am not ashamed of the gospel of Christ: for it is the power of God unto salvation to every one that believeth" (Rom. 1:16).

Wherever the Dodgers would send me, I always joined a local church. While playing for the Silver Sox in Reno, Nevada, it was the Sparks Church. The pastor had served for more than four years without a vacation to his home state of Arkansas. Since the church was small, funds for such a trip were not available. This began to weigh upon my mind.

So, one day in the clubhouse I made an announcement to the team as we were suiting up before an evening game, "My preacher needs a vacation, and I'm taking up an offering." Out came my ball cap, and right then and there the players chipped in $160 to send him to Arkansas.

I remember Bob Gialombardo quipped, "Hey Minton, I'm a Catholic, just pass me up!" Of course, Bob was jesting.

I responded, "I'll tell you what, you get an offering going for one of the priests, and I'll support it."

One year the Dodgers sent me to the great Northwest

of Montana, Utah, and Idaho. It was there in that great expansive area that I first became acquainted with mission churches. Up to that time I had always worshiped the Lord where the buildings were large and beautiful. But the great Northwest showed me pioneer missions first hand. It wasn't long before I was a member of a struggling little band of believers of the First Southern Baptist Church of Great Falls, Montana. Here I saw what it meant to believe, even though it was not the most popular thing to do.

In Reno, Nevada, when I was playing my third year of baseball, my wife and I joined the little Sparks Baptist mission church. The pastor worked at night for the post office and did his best to pastor the church. It was a struggle for the little church to pay the pastor enough so he could minister full time.

As was my custom, I tithed my first baseball check. That afternoon the pastor telephoned and very politely asked, "Say, young man, are you a tither?"

"Yes," I replied. "I have been tithing since I began playing baseball several years ago."

"That's wonderful," he exclaimed. "Now I can quit my night job and become a full-time pastor!"

That experience made my baseball income an added blessing to me. Our church Sunday School nearly doubled in attendance that summer, because our pastor could spend more time ministering to the people.

I knew in my heart at age eleven that God had called me to preach, but I wanted to play baseball, too. I promised the Lord if I could play a few years of pro ball, then I'd preach.

My preaching came sooner than I had expected. The

very first year at spring training in Vero Beach, Florida, the pastor, Rev. Rogers of the First Baptist Church, announced in church that they needed someone to preach at the Rose Park mission.

Don Demeter and my twin brother, Fred, heard the preacher's words and immediately Fred said to me, "Hey, Frank, here is your chance. You preach, and I'll lead the singing."

Then Don Demeter chimed in, "And I'll take up the offering."

After the service, we enthusiastically approached Rev. Rogers with our plans.

"Well, if you think you can handle it," came his reluctant answer.

That next Sunday three baseball players had charge of the service in that little mission with a dirt floor. Fred sang from the top of his lungs as forty others chimed in. True to his word, Don Demeter took up the offering and served as our lone usher. Very nervous-like and with haltering words, I preached, using my notes that I had written on some Brookly Dodger stationery. To our surprise and the congregation's, we survived with no casualties.

For the next three Sundays, we took our places as preacher, music leader, and usher. It was an unexpected pleasure for three baseball "rookies" at spring training.

This past summer I visited Vero Beach after twenty years. The spring training camp now has first clas motel-type quarters. All the facilities are much improved at Dodgertown. It was great to walk on to the practice diamond and reminisce. But there was a special place in my heart as I drove by the little lot where the Rose Park mission used to stand. In its place today stands a large, strong church edifice.

Most all games in the minor leagues are played under the lights at night. This gives a ball player time on his hands during the day and especially while on the road. It doesn't take a player long to get bored sitting around a hotel lobby or window shopping.

Some pick up a hobby, become afternoon movie matinee watchers, or play pool. When I first arrived in a town, I would thumb through the Yellow Pages and locate the Southern Baptist preacher. It wouldn't be long before we would have lunch together and talk about the pastor's work.

On one occasion in Twin Falls, Idaho, the church was constructing a small building. In fact, the pastor, Rev. Harold Dillman, was literally constructing it himself. My twin brother and I decided to help, so for two afternoons, we dug footings and poured concrete. When it came time for the game, we could hardly drag ourselves onto the field. Our hands were so blistered that holding a bat became painful. Lou Rochelle, our manager, couldn't figure out why we seemed to have suddenly come up with aches and pains. But it was for the kingdom of God, and we felt it was worth it.

Because God had given us twins the ability to play professional baseball, we had a strong desire to use our talent for the Lord. As ball players we met hundreds of people who were willing to let us talk with them. So, we ordered 2,000 tracts called "God's Simple Plan of Salvation" and handed them out in every city we played in. Oftentimes just before we left the visiting team's clubhouse, we would put a tract in every locker. The word finally got around the league, "Well, the Dodgers and the Mintons were here last. I see they are trying to convert us."

Many times when I was pitching, I would hear the opposing bench holler out, "You'd better pray, preacher, because tonight you're gonna get bombed!" And sometimes they were right.

Sad but true, on a few occasions my baseball blood got the best of me. It happened in, Pocatello, Idaho. I had been knocked out of the box in the seventh inning. We had been leading 3 to 1, but I had finally run out of gas. As I sat the bench, the opposing pitcher by the name of Simone began to make a few choice remarks. Soon he and I were in a loud yelling match, and before either one of us had time to think, we were going at it with our fists flying.

It looked like a ferocious fight, but it was more the swing-and-miss variety, which soon became a poor wrestling match at first base. I do remember that Simone bit me on the arm, and I guess I had it coming 'cause I was pulling his hair. As umpires, managers, and other players came diving into the foray, it almost got out of hand. Small fights broke out everywhere on the field and in the grandstands, too. Within a few moments, peace was restored. But just as Simone and I were ejected from the game, Simone busted me with a parting fist that gave a real shiner to my right eye.

After the game, this "baseball preacher" sure felt ashamed. I tried to give an apologetic speech concerning my behavior, but my faithful combatants all cheerfully drowned out my efforts with their rendition of the song, "For He's a Jolly Good Fellow."

The next day I was interviewed on television, black eye

and all. Of course, they were interested in the fight and my reactions as a "one-day-to-be preacher."

"Well," I said, "the only thing I ever got out of a fight is this black eye. But since you mentioned me as a preacher, if I can't preach Christ to them, I'll beat the devil out of 'em."

One of the biggest disappointments that I found in professional baseball was the importance the management placed upon alcoholic beverages. After every game the team won, free beer was placed in the center of the clubhouse for all to drink. Since I didn't drink, I would request a Coke but was always informed that I'd have to buy my own.

Baseball and beer do not mix. Alcohol and athletics are not compatible. The last place the manager wants to see his player in is a bar.

To place alcoholic beverages as a symbol of success is phony. It never builds an athlete, but actually slows him down. To see Hall of Famers promote the sale of beer on television commercials gives evidence of the inroads big beer money has made into baseball.

Possibly the most notorious publicity to low-rate the game is the cork-popping, champagne-pouring scenes as a club celebrates winning the pennant or World Series. Baseball and booze are incompatible in the locker room of the players, or in the stands of the fans. In 1974, Cleveland experienced a full-scale riot when the fans were given free beer for attending a game. Of course, the beer industry quickly labeled the incident as unrelated to the beer-promoting scheme. But just the same, Cleveland didn't repeat the mistake during the 1975 season.

While we were on the road—playing in Stockton, California—a bat boy informed me that a far, distant relative of mine named Minton was in the grandstand. He pointed to the man who was near the third base line. Eagerly, I jogged over to where the other Minton was sitting.

As I neared the stands, I could see plainly that he was obnoxiously drunk. Waving his arms like a windmill and sounding out like a fog horn, he yelled out to me.

"Hey, Minton, we have the same name, so play a good game, 'cause I don't want to be embarrassed."

These words, of course, sent a roar of laughter throughout the crowd in that section of the stadium.

Batboys were always good friends of the ball club. But some were more special than others. On occasions I would talk with them about Jesus Christ and give them tracts to read.

While driving through Oklahoma several years after my baseball career, I stopped to get gasoline at a service station. I gave my credit card to the young college student who looked at the card with a special interest.

"Say, are you the same Frank Minton who pitched at Shawnee for the Dodgers?"

"I sure am," came my surprised reply.

"Well, shake hands with your batboy, and you'll be glad to know that I'm a Christian now and a member of First Baptist Church here in town."

Sometimes it was difficult to witness directly to the players about Jesus. A few thought I was a religious freak and really poured on the ridicule. But generally as the season wore on, the jokes and unpleasant remarks gave way to acceptance. In fact, almost always each player in his own way would get around to show his personal interest. They came around because game after game, win or lose, they knew I still believed.

There wasn't a bigger heckler about Fred and my images as Christians than an outfielder we named "Suitcase" Simpson. He got that nickname after the famous major leaguer by the same name.

During the first inning in Gainesville, Texas, Fred laid a bunt down the first base line. In charged the hulking first baseman. The ball rolled so close to the chalk lines that Fred and the huge baseman collided. It was like a Mack truck hitting a Volkswagen.

Poor Fred laid stretched out halfway between the batter's box and first base. He was completely knocked out by the collision.

"Suitcase" Simpson suddenly jumped out of the dugout, ran over to where Fred was lying, and intently bent over him. Moments later Fred began to move and moan.

Then the surprised Simpson jumped up and came running over the dugout, yelling, "He didn't cuss, he didn't cuss!"

Playing baseball on Sunday was always a nagging spiritual problem. Before Fred and I signed our second-year contracts, we asked Brooklyn if we could keep Sunday as a day of worship and not play. Dick Walsh, then general manager of the minor leagues, sent a three-page letter giving admiration to our request but tactfully declining it.

But Sunday baseball continued to be a problem to me. During my last year at Reno, Nevada, I had a 10-1 won-loss pitching record going. Then, the next three pitching starts on Sunday, I lost.

During the game of my third loss, Ray Perry, my manager, came to the mound and said, "You call it religion, and I call it psychology, but either way you can't pitch for me on Sunday again." Ray kept his word, and I was grateful to him for it. I always believed that deep down in Ray's heart, he knew it was God's doing, too.

God granted me three of the happiest years of my life in baseball. But I knew he had called me to preach the gospel, so today, like the Apostle Paul, "I press toward the mark for the prize of the high calling of God in Christ Jesus" (Phil. 3:14).

After the contracts came out for my fourth year of baseball, I spent a long evening in the home of my pastor, Rev. Gordon Dorian, in Wichita, Kansas, discussing and praying about baseball. That night I made my final decision to leave baseball and enter the ministry. It wasn't long after that I realized my hometown, Wichita, Kansas, in itself was a mission field for God.

Immediately my wife and I laid plans for the construction of a new house in a large unchurched area. Meeting in our new home with seventeen people, the Tyler Road Baptist Church was born. The baseball days were officially over, and a new God-called career had begun.

After twenty years, as I look back at my unknown baseball career, it isn't the thrills of the diamond that linger closest to my heart. The most impressionable experiences were those that involved the kingdom of God. Runs, hits, and errors have their place, but they are not in the same league with the prayers, witnessing, and walking with God that took place some twenty years ago.